Divergent Terror:
At the Crossroads of
Queerness and Horror

Edited by W. Dale Jordan

OFF LIMITS
PRESS

Table of Contents

I am Ready to Communicate With You Now: An Introduction

When I was asked to write an introduction to the book in your hands, my mind immediately—based off the title alone—spiralled into queer theory. But upon finishing *Divergent Terror*, theory didn't seem to matter much anymore. I had nothing to say. Nothing to add. This is a book that invites you to sit back and listen, to revel in the magic of its mystery (not its secrets, but we'll get to that), and to learn from voices that are not your own. To some degree, I am the most unqualified person to write an introduction to such a book. I'm not sure anyone is qualified to do this.

And quite possibly that's a very good thing.

What *Divergent Terror* did do, however, was invite me to share my own story, to explore the relationship between my identity and the horror genre I love so dearly because it is the genre that has loved me back. How could this book *not* offer such an invitation, considering the richness of the voices within? Frankly, I was inspired.

In lieu of an introduction in the formal sense, allow me to indulge and accept *Divergent Terror's* invitation. The following questions bubble to the surface.

What were the first times I saw my own identity represented in other creative mediums—be those mediums motion pictures, television, or books? Was that representation coded or overt? How far did I have to reach to pretzel myself into the shape of something 'other' so as to feel less alone in a darkened theatre, when all around me kids who felt the world differently saw the best parts of themselves characterized so clearly? What muscles developed in my pursuit for identification? What did I learn along the way? Which of those lessons, what muscles, do I continue to flex today both as a consumer of art and as a creator?

The answers to these questions were preceded by something I've long thought, but never actualised before now:

You don't have to know the ins and outs—even the vague shape of your identity, let alone know how to harness your energy and potential—to know that you are not seeing yourself in the media you consume and love. You know this, even when you don't *know*. There really is no other way to say it than that. You just *know*. Even when you're young. Before you come of age and understand your sexuality.

Growing up, I was a kind of socially amorphous kid. I was liked by many but not fully embraced anywhere. I was seen as funny by most and worthy of hate by a select few. The weird guy. The curious one. A creative in a sea of sportspeople, scraping by in an environment where merit was measured by how fast you coursed a 100-metre pool or how far you threw a javelin or in how many tackles you could take on the field before your bones started to splinter. I was street smart but found it difficult to meet tertiary expectations—so hardly an academic. I was an oil slick on a very old, tradition-heavy sea, floating about yet never truly mixing, a slick that caught the light in ways that made people both attracted to and sometimes fearful of me. I wasn't unhappy. However, I lived in fear of making anyone around me *unhappy*. That pressure was one I forced upon myself. At times, the weight was so heavy I thought it would kill me. In many ways, I haven't changed since then.

2

I still search for myself in art. In horror. And even when I find it, I seem to want to seek more. To seek it on a deeper level. To find reflections of myself in the absolute pitch dark, in surrealism and the bizarre and the obtuse. Searches for myself aren't as arduous these days as they used to be. But the muscle I mentioned before needs to flex. That is why—even though representation has come so far—I still seek metaphors to feed off. Ray Bradbury spoke of the nourishment of metaphors, and I wholeheartedly agree. I'd *also* say that seeing queers in movies and television does not always equate to representation. I'm not just a flag. Not a box for someone to tick. I have meaning and depth and complexity. I'm not your cute panda. I have issues and carry inherited trauma, and the indulgence of that trauma (I'm sorry) is in many ways how I honour those giants upon whose shoulders I proudly stand. I am not nourished by the outline of virtue and appearance. And that's because I am a messy creature of desire, want, regret, guilt, shame, kink, and curiosity. I am glorious, hideous, godly, shit, masochistic, giving. I am selfish. I am selfless. I am all the things at once. I am not what a lot of queer characters tend to be in these sanitized, Mickey Mousified, corporately marginalized times. I am not a Secret in disguise.

I am a human being.

No wonder I saw myself in the cinematic stars that others saw as monstrous. I am John Merrick in David Lynch's *The Elephant Man*, cowering in the public bathroom with a sack over my head, suffocating so others can comfortably exist, screaming at those who wish to force me into their own image (which is to say, power over me with Godly intent), begging for empathy. *See me.* See

3

me as I really am. Trace the outline of me in the dark and discover how similar we are.

The two of us together in a moment of convergence, not divergence.

I rarely see myself in these clichéd big or small screen Stepford Queers, the wind-up toys that march about to make others feel better, or to meet a quota, or to get a laugh, or to be killed off without ceremony. More frequently, more deeply, I see more of myself in what is *not* said, in what is *not* shown. Maybe I'm just old fashioned. Maybe that muscle both helps me create enriched fiction whilst also holding me back.

This is not to say representation does not and should not matter. It *very* much does. If it is a solution I'm seeking here, it is that I hope the future of queer horror incorporates the visibility of modern representation whilst embracing the chaotic, sometimes villainous, often allegorical full-bodied artistry of the past. Excitingly, I think this is happening in the independent horror fiction scene. A colorful pushback against the blandification of the industry. Let us hope that the big publishing houses, the television streamers, and film companies/distributors follow suit. And if not, then let's double down within this space. Keep independent art punk as fuck and may our stories—and the *way* we tell our stories—bring them to us instead of us to them. But let's not forget the power of metaphor along the way. By nature, the metaphoric is inclusive. We need not all be alone always.

I speak only of my personal experience, my own wishes and hopes. However, as I mentioned above, *Divergent Terror* is the kind of book that invites you to share your own relationship with the horror genre.

Speak to me, the book says. *Someone out there is listening.*

And not just your relationship with the genre, but your relationship with its future. To go forward, though, we must look back. The book has invited me to do that, too.

Who was I when I fell in love with horror?

I was (and still am) The Elephant Man screaming out his identity. Even though I don't want to admit it, there's probably a lot of Uncle Frank from Clive Barker's *Hellraiser* in me—I am imperfect and will cower when I should be strong, and in my pursuits stretch my skin over the shapes of others to survive. I am not above jealousy and the stab of rejection—Alex telling Dan that she will not be ignored in *Fatal Attraction.* I am The Second Mrs. De Winter, repulsed at myself for letting the long-dead Rebecca cuckold me in my own home, making me feel like I don't belong. I am often a creature of rage, Cujo chasing rabbits until that rabid bat came along and stripped away an ability to control, physiology warping around a virus, driven mad by noise and movement, and offended by the visage of the perfect family unit (joke is on both Cujo and me here—just ask Donna in her broken-down Pinto about the perfect family). I am Dennis in Christine, terribly (and quietly) hurt by how Arnie Cunningham has abandoned me for that red Plymouth Fury, unable to tell Arnie how much I love and miss him. I am Carrie White on her knees with tears in her eyes asking: *Why didn't you tell me, Momma?* I am sometimes charismatic and powerful, but that charisma can be as destructive as it is healing—the yellow mist creeping from the earth in James Herbert's *The Fog,* bringing forth appetites for primal destruction. I am Father Karras in *The Exorcist,* who must rekindle his faith if he's to have a chance in hell of defeating a servant of Hell. I am

5

Laura Palmer in *Twin Peaks*, doomed to die again and again in a cosmic cycle, those transfixed by my murder more at home with my darker self with each iteration, the plastic in which my body was wrapped becoming more transparent. I am the hope of the sky in the opening of *Blue Velvet* (perfect skies inherently invite tragedy), am the idealism of the picket fence, am the liar of the over-manicured lawn, and I am the beetles swarming beneath the soil. I am many things at once.

I am Cole Sear.

The year is 1999. I am in the ninth grade. I am at the movies watching M. Night Shyamalan's *The Sixth Sense* starring Bruce Willis, Toni Collette (who I'd long seen myself in since her star-making turn in 1994's *Muriel's Wedding*, a film I can recite verbatim), and an incredible— even prodigious—Haley Joel Osment as the young and tortured Cole Sear, blessed (or cursed) with the titular ability of seeing and feeling what others cannot.

We're almost at the very end of the film. Cole, the eleven-year-old, is in the passenger's seat of his mother's car. His mother, Lynn (Collette), is behind the wheel, straining to see the source of the traffic jam keeping them in place. "Geeze," Lynn says. "I hope nobody got hurt." We suspect someone has been hurt because this is horror.

Cole turns to his mother after a long pause, and with the sad courage only dread can bring, says to her: "I'm ready to communicate with you now."

When Lynn seeks clarification, Cole simply says he wants to tell her his secrets.

It was then I started to squirm in my cinema seat.

Because sometimes you know things even when you don't know. I wouldn't come out to my family for a few more years. To some degree, I only partially knew – or had a word for – the ways in which I was different. But my body knew. And my body reacted in that cinema. It was a deep feeling. Primal. I was afraid.

Cole informs his mother that someone did die in an accident up ahead. And that the dead woman, a bicyclist, is standing right beside his window. We, the viewer, see this gaunt, pale woman bleeding from beneath the helmet that did not save her. Lynn, understandably, does not believe her son at first. But Cole (I'm emotional just typing this now) holds his ground. The child pushes back on the rationality of adulthood, personified in the one person he loves more than anyone: his mother in her orange turtleneck, her eyes widening as he tells her about an event that only she could possibly know about. Evidence that cannot be debunked.

"Cole, you're scaring me," she says.

What person coming out didn't hear those words—you're scaring me—from those they loved? Or see it in their face. *Scared because they care.*

This scene has the shape and feeling of the coming out experience. It's right there in all its messiness and anxiety. The child who has made the choice to let those who think they know them best know that not only do they not…that the parts they identify with the most strongly (namely, their expectations of and for us) are already dead. Really, learning and accepting your sexuality, your identity, your queerness, is in many ways a death.

"Ghosts," Cole says. Ha. In my ears, he might as well have been saying "gay." "What are you thinking mother? Are you thinking I'm a freak?"

AARON DRIES

I cannot tell you how my physical body still reacts to watching Toni Collette turning in her seat towards him, almost angry and defiant, and telling her son to look at her face. "I would never think that about you." Beat. "Ever." It also makes me grateful. Not everyone gets to receive that look. I know far too many who haven't.

And then Cole drops the emotional A-bomb. He tells her that Grandma, his mother's mother, says hi. Lynn is offended by this at first. If her son is lying, this is a low blow. We, the viewer, know he's telling the truth, that he's being honest for the first time.

But Lynn needs proof. Who can blame her, really?

So, Cole gives it to her. "She wants me to tell you that she saw you dance."

Toni Collette, my beloved Muriel, glares at her son, all motherly annoyance burned away in the heat of that bomb. This raw shock has made a daughter of her for the first time in a long time. They are now, finally, truly, communicating. Cole elaborates. Lynn and her mother had a fight before her dance recital—one of those childhood memories we never forget, the little betrayals that haunt us decades later. And then Cole gives his mother the answer to an unknown question. Grandma's answer. Two words.

"Every day," he says, furrowing his brow. "What did you ask?"

Choking back tears, hand to her neck, moved beyond comprehension, Lynn equals her son's bravery and tells him, voice quivering: "Do I … make her proud?"

That this scene ends in an embrace means so much to me.

Surely, I am not the only one who feels this way, who was nourished, and healed, by the metaphor. This is my divergent horror. There in 1999, the me who didn't even know who I was found hope in the horror genre. If this scene were to conversely feature a young son actually coming out to his mother—I do not think it would have resonated with me as strongly. I may have even pushed away from the film as it triggered the kind of cringe that comes with seeing yourself too closely in too bright a light. These scenes (and I've seen many) strike me as being too conclusive. Less a conversation than a statement (though the statement is often powerful). For me, I see myself more deeply through allegory, through the oblique, in that which invites me to communicate with me on common, often frightening ground.

Metaphor. Metaphors are mysteries for us all to solve. They commune.

Ray Bradbury was right.

All these years later, like Cole, I still speak with the dead. My novella, *Dirty Heads*, is about this very subject. The dead person I grew up thinking I would become lingers with me. The dead person my parents thought I would be. The dead people my friends, if they were my friends (some abandoned me after I came out) expected me to align with (again, the Godly ego that prowls small towns, cities, and suburbia). I do not fear these ghosts as I once did. I am on the other side of much of this because I am one of the lucky ones. Those who love me acknowledged the dead parts, my ghosts, and learned to love what was always there. Those who could not do this experienced my death over and over again in their hearts until they could not bear to be around me a second longer. Their pain drove them away from me. I don't hate them for leaving. I still grieve their loss.

More ghosts.

Ghosts everywhere.

I am ready to communicate with you now.

The authors within this book are not Secrets. We are *Mysteries*. It is important to remember the distinction. Secrets are things we create to protect ourselves and others. Fuck that noise. Mysteries, on the other hand, are cosmic and eternal, and we rarely know why they exist or where they come from. There is much to learn from the mysteries of this world.

So, let's listen.

Because we are ready.

Aaron Dries

Canberra, Australia, November 2022

Bihexuality and *The Craft*
Anna Orridge

The scratched old wooden table in our school yard was normally used to sell sticky buns and doughnuts at break time. But it was also the exact length of the average 12-year-old girl.

Most days, one of us would lie on that table. I always longed to be chosen, but I was never pushy enough about it, and it was always someone else's turn.

Everyone would put two fingers underneath the prone girl, her eyes closed, lids quivering.

In *The Craft*, when the four witches try out the game, there's that same sense of elicit thrill. 'Put your fingers where?' asks Nancy, when Sarah explains the game to her, making an unmistakable gesture with her fingers, to uproarious cackling from the others.

And at school, we used the same words as the girls in the film.

Light as a feather, stiff as a board.

The chant had an odd, soothing tension. We whispered it, slowly getting louder and louder. The girl lying before us would always rise, quite suddenly, with little effort from any of us doing the lifting.

Levitation never happened, though, like it did in the film. We just lowered her quietly down. It was odd. There was never any giggling or astonishment. Just this odd air of almost sacrosanct wonder.

*　　*　　*

Lots of girls at school had a flutter with the occult. A fair few cracked out the Ouija board at sleepovers, although I was never brave enough.

The Ouija board doesn't make an appearance in *The Craft*. Spirits, in fact, seem oddly lacking in presence. There's a scene in which Nancy invokes Manon. The spirit does not make an appearance himself, though. Instead, we have Nancy walking on water toward the other girls, who watch her with an odd sort of blankness. Raving, she collapses in ecstasy before the beached body of a gleaming whale, one of the many Manon has apparently offered her as a sacrifice.

But Manon is very much an absentee landlord sort of deity. Nancy, in a fit of pantheistic zeal, says that he's everywhere. But that kind of means he's also nowhere, doesn't it? All the real thrill from magic in *The Craft* comes from transformation and mutability: exactly the power (and danger) our culture ascribes to bisexuality.

I recognise the exhilaration of transformation. I felt it the morning after I did, for the first time, return the gaze of another woman. We took it from there, and she didn't hold back.

I didn't even feel quite the same, just walking to the supermarket for a few bottles of orange juice. It was probably about as close as I have ever got to the insouciant confidence of *The Craft* girls in the film poster, all in the black mini-skirts of the era, hips atilt, heads thrown back, doing a sexy-menacing catwalk strut towards the camera. I fancied there was a directness and audacity in my gaze that had never been there before.

The exhilaration didn't last, of course, and neither did the courage. Even as I write this essay, I'm nervous about the prospect of friends and family seeing it, although I suspect many of them know I'm not straight.

*   *   *

Shortly after their ritual binding as a coven, the Craft girls decide to stretch their magical wings by doing glamour spells. 'Glamour,' here, refers to a spell that creates a temporary illusion. But there is plenty of glamour of the more conventional kind in the scene.

For 14-year-old me, sleepovers meant naff pyjamas and giggling and some back-biting gossip in the dark. In *The Craft*, it's all conspiratorial feminine joy. Everything's muted and sensual – the candles, the flowers, the soft fabrics, and the spa-style music with faint vocals. There's that joy in touch when Sarah runs her hands over her face and hair, transforming it from light brown to blond.

Nancy uses almost exactly the same gesture later in the movie when she transforms herself into Sarah for the benefit of a lovelorn and horny Chris. Nancy's heavily black-lined eyes and sharp features make way for Sarah's soft-focus, dimpled beauty. 'Make love to me, Chris,' said with an edge of mocking bravado that is definitely not Sarah's. But Chris, being the dumb jock, falls for it, of course.

*   *   *

A friend, perched on one of the ancient school desks, read out the newspaper listing. "Four teenage girls, banished from the coolest cliques at high school, turn to the occult for solace and distraction..." She looked up and grinned. "Yep. Sounds like us."

We laughed, but in a forlorn way. We were genuine outsiders. Not edgy, gorgeous, defiant outsiders decked out in Goth chic with an achingly cool Indie soundtrack. We were geeks before Geek found its way onto T-shirts and gained cultural cache. We were also British, in a single-sex school, so a lot of the American high school movie tropes (braying soccer jocks, rows of lockers, massive mixed-gender house parties) did not even bear the dimmest of resemblances to our lives.

Still, it was the only movie we were likely to be able to gain admittance to at the cinema that wasn't for kids. So that was our choice for my friend's fourteenth birthday party. And we sat in a gaggle with our popcorn, lapping it all up.

*   *   *

Seeing *The Craft* was quite a big deal for me. My mother didn't approve of horror movies. I'd cast many a yearning look at the Horror section of the local Blockbuster, with all those glaring red dot 18 badges.

I remember the *Hellraiser* cover in particular and the white, snarling face with its grid of pins. My mother would never let me hire one of these out, but I think I intuited this genre had the potential not only to thrill but to give voice to subversive longings I couldn't yet name. LGBTQ people know all the gradations of fear, especially that apprehension of being watched, which runs through the entire genre.

In 80s British suburbia, there was nothing more brutally mocked than queerness. One of my primary school teachers was known to live with another woman. My only real memory of her is a pretty dreadful one. Our class was doing a cycling proficiency course, and she decided to test whether we could all tell our right from our left. Unfortunately, this was a skill I hadn't yet mastered.

She shouted out 'Left' and 'Right,' and each time we had to raise the correct hand. After several tries, it became apparent that I was the only one who was dithering and trying to follow everyone else. So, Miss Barrett got everyone else to sit down and barked commands at me until the class was in an uproar. Eventually, I stopped putting my hands up and simply stared at her. I'd like to portray this as defiance, but it was more silent pleading. I was a diffident child. She let me sit down eventually, numb with humiliation.

Just before we packed up for the day, the boy opposite leaned over. He made an L shape with the thumb and forefinger of his left hand. He winked at me. "That's how I remember it." And, from that day onwards, it was how I remembered it too. He was a better teacher than she was.

In retrospect, it's almost too perfect, too 'pat' a childhood memory for a bisexual woman: the wavering between two opposites, the queasy public shaming.

I'm aware there are far greater cruelties you can suffer as a child than this, but it's still lodged in my memory, perhaps simply because it was so gratuitous. I was a painfully quiet girl, so she couldn't have been acting out of frustration or vengeance. She was doing it for a laugh.

Anyway, Miss Barrett and her girlfriend were themselves the butt of endless jokes: open, jeering ones from kids and nod-nod-wink-wink ones from adults. 'Barrett and Berger are lesbos!" one of the neighbourhood boys hooted, making scissors out of the fore and middle fingers of both his hands and interlocking them. I had no idea what that gesture signified, but I was sure to laugh along as riotously as everyone else. Perhaps more so. I was entitled to mock this woman who had abused her authority over me. But, even then, it was combined with a guilt that nipped at my peripheries.

I'd always linger over the magazines near the top shelf at the newsagent, showing women with breasts or rear exposed and the merest slips of thongs to cover them, their heads tilted to one side in feigned diffidence. They held for me a curious allure that I couldn't yet articulate.

"Don't look at smut like that, love!" a man once guffawed at me. I scuttled out of the shop, flustered.

*   *   *

The Craft has long been identified as a queer movie. Take that scene where the four girls set off on a bus to an idyllic rural enclave and that gif-able moment when the solicitous bus driver tells them to look out for weirdos. Nancy tips her sunglasses at him. "We ARE the weirdos, Mister."

It's clearly meant to signify a retreat to a safe space for queer youth, where they engage in a communal ritual of 'coming out.'

The camera gently glides round them as they hold the dagger to each other's throat and promise to enter the coven "with perfect love and perfect trust" before coming to rest on a singularly intense Sarah. It's hardly subtle. I mean, "I drink of my sisters," for fuck's sake? But as a teenager, I didn't pick up on any of this.

Even though I was, by then, fearfully aware of my attraction to girls, I did not sympathise with the proudly 'out' girl of the film, Nancy. Instead, I identified with Sarah, the insipid lead. Yes, Sarah, who opted for the obsession of a leering straight-from-central-casting jock when she could have had the pungent rewards of power, beauty, or revenge that the other girls chose.

I was no Nancy. I was not even much of a Sarah. If I had anything in common with any of the girls, it would probably have been Bonnie – her initial diffidence, her desire to please and appease. I even had that same habit of letting my long hair hang in front of my face. I can remember the taunt I once overheard in the school yard.

"God, I hate that girl. She's so droopy."

(I can't help but laugh at the fact we're expected to code Bonnie as ugly at that stage in the movie. A slight slouch and some strategically placed strands of hair were never going to make Neve Campbell anything less than gorgeous.)

I could identify, too, with her fraught relationship with beauty. When she covers up her extensive burns with enveloping clothes, she's treated with a mixture of contempt, indifference, and derision.

But as soon as she marches regally into class, magically free of burns, made-up, and in revealing clothes, she finds herself berated for narcissism.

I never had any disfigurement, but I remember the yearning for magazine-perfect looks. Instead, I had braces and spent a lot of time covering my smile with a hand. If I spent a morning trying on various outfits and twirling in front of the mirror, I'd be mocked by my parents for "flitting around like a butterfly." Any relaxation into baggy clothes and scrubbed face, on the other hand, would be met by tutting about me "not making the best of myself."

Incidentally, one thing that stands out about The Craft is its take on feminism and the validity of female adolescent anger. Nancy's screaming at Chris before she sends him tumbling to his death from a window.

"You don't exist! You are nothing! You are shit! You don't exist. The only way you know how to treat women is by treating them like whores! Well, you're the whore!"

Some pretty strong sauce, that, decades before #MeToo.

The Craft has its problematic elements, as do almost all teen movies of the era. Rochelle, the one Black character, is defined to far too great an extent by the gross racist abuse directed at her early in the film. The actor, Rachel True, does her best to inject warmth and nuance into the role, but she's the only girl denied the humanizing presence of at least one parent. Rochelle can't even enjoy a full-blooded vengeance against the girl who taunts her and abuses her. Instead, Rochelle is made to sympathise with that "racist piece of bleach blond shit" as her locks fall out. She even ends up watching her own hair fall out in the later part of the film, albeit only temporarily, after a glamour spell cast by the morally unimpeachable Sarah.

Of course, all of this is pretty standard in Hollywood films. So many of the famous cinematic quartets of my childhood included a token, undeveloped character of colour. Take Winston in Ghostbusters. Little white 14-year-old me was quite oblivious to all that at the time. I'm not proud of it.

*   *   *

The movie's climax sees Nancy return to Sarah's house after an attempt to stage her former friend's suicide. Instead of a corpse, Nancy encounters deserted rooms and silence. Then, when she looks around, her own reflection in the mirror turns into Sarah, who plucks herself out of the mirror world to seize her nemesis by the shoulder.

"Why aren't you dead?" demands Nancy.

In return, Sarah apes her sadistic, deadpan delivery.

"What happened to Rochelle and Bonnie? They rushed out of here without even saying goodbye. It's bad manners."

Of course, even at this moment of power, she can't quite catch Nancy's wit, elan, or ferocity. Nobody can.

Fairuza Balk's performance as Nancy is probably one of the most remarkable in US teen cinema. You can read Nancy's character arc as a simple descent into insanity, and I think that might even be what the scriptwriters intended. Sarah, at one point, tells the white witch in the New Age shop that summoning Manon drove Nancy mad.

But Balk's performance is so much more than that. Many of her scenes are joyful scenery chewing. The thing is, though, she has a whole spectrum of emotions for you to marvel at in that process of dramatic mastication. She has that deliriously, gloriously mobile face. In a moment, she can switch from charm to deranged ecstasy to sheer snarling rage. The real terror in the movie does not lie in cockroaches crawling out of sinks or fingers turning into snakes. It lies in the moments between those moods.

*   *   *

Nancy reminds me of Dawn.

Dawn was not a Goth, but she was sure as hell channelling a lot of the indomitable Nancy spirit. She had long flame-red hair and wore her regulation grey pleated skirt unfashionably long. But in our single-sex school, where the only openly gay teacher would regularly get notes stuck to his back with messages like 'I like it doggy style' scrawled on them, Dawn dared to be openly, exuberantly lesbian.

There were breathless stories of her getting up on her desk and noisily snogging a picture of Billie Piper at her gauche pop star stage. She was whispered about and treated with contempt, but she slung all the mockery gleefully back in everyone's faces.

I, on the other hand, was furtive. Any glances of yearning at other girls were taken as briefly as possible. I could never enjoy hugs the way my classmates did, with noisy, squealing abandon.

You can see that same flicker of guilt and fear of discovery in Sarah when Bonnie catches her doing some sneaky telekinesis with a pencil in a French class. The camera glides down from Sarah's intent green eyes to the slowly rotating pencil. We hear the creak of lead boring into wood, improbably loud, and then Bonnie's slight double gasp. The pencil tumbles. Both girls dart glances at one another. I know that odd sensory clarity and the panicked evasion of eye contact all too well.

*   *   *

Just after graduating from university, I was at an intensive teacher training course in Spain. It was just a month-long, and all the trainees were accommodated in a single, large flat near the language centre.

One fellow trainee was a statuesque woman of twenty-seven from New Zealand. Blond, with glorious marsh-green eyes, she was showily "hippie," an almost comical stereotype in retrospect. She sold prayer mats from Goa and smoked joints almost continuously. When we had drunken sing-a-longs, she'd join in, but had one of the worst, most discordant voices I'd ever heard. Still, you couldn't fault her gusto.

To a rather sheltered twenty-one-year-old, she seemed the epitome of the free spirit. I fancied her, of course.

One evening in town, in a taxi after wine and a meal, she told me I looked cute, like a pixie. I suppose she was referring to my slightly sticky-out ears. But I've always had a broad, sanguine face that is anything but elfin. It was an odd thing to say. She held my gaze with a mischievous, lascivious intensity. I, of course, looked down. It was a pattern of cowardice that held on for a very long time.

A few years later, I shared a flat with a girl I nursed an almost Petrarchan admiration for. She had long dark brown curls, huge blue eyes and a rangy, long-limbed figure. I'd lie in bed and think of her freckles and her huge smile, but there was no flirtation. In all honesty, I think I was as much enamoured with her inaccessibility as I was with her.

*   *   *

"What's the deal?" Rochelle asks, as she, Bonnie, and Nancy hover several feet above the ground, leering down at a weeping Sarah. 'Why doesn't she use magic on us?"

"Because she's WEAK!" shrieks Nancy. 'Weak, weak, weak. Oh God." She reaches up to tug on that wild black hair that's doing a slow-motion dance of its own throughout the movie. "You're so disgusting."

I feel that line in my gut.

The woman I finally slept with after years of prevarication remained a friend afterwards. We didn't really talk about the one-night stand ever again. But once, when we were drinking with some other friends at her house, she got talking about the female actors she fancied. I fell silent.

She leaned over me with an odd sort of leer. "Hey, Anna. You're quiet. You must like some of these babes. We both KNOW you do."

I simply stared at the rising bubbles of my strawberry gin and stammered something, ashamed of my own shame.

I came across a meme recently featuring Nancy sporting one of her more unhinged, Joker-style smiles.

"Are you a good witch or a bad witch? Honey, I'm both. I'm bihexual."

Nancy's killing of Chris seems to be as much about jealousy as anger. She resents how Sarah's attention is being drawn from her and from the coven, but she also enjoys the sex with Chris before Sarah bursts in on them.

To me, though, her aggression towards Sarah reads more as gay suspicion of bisexuality.

There's always that taunt that bi people can't make up their minds, or even worse, we want the main course security of straightness but the dissident spice of queerness as a side. And that's what I hear in Nancy's disdain for Sarah's dithering over witchcraft, her cowardice, and her refusal to give herself completely to the coven and to Manon.

*   *   *

You see a few glints of vulnerability in Nancy – that genuine hurt in her downward glance when she tells Sarah that she should stay away from Chris because he spreads disease, and she should know.

But Nancy is almost always in control. Even when she is screaming at Chris before murdering him, hair flying round her head as her feet skim the floor, gliding towards him in a controlled manner that belies her seeming mania. A moment later, after the grim thud of Chris's body, she is calm. It's a performance within a performance.

This is what makes the ending of the movie so deeply unsatisfactory. Nancy ends up a sub-*One Flew Over the Cuckoo's Nest* cliché, raving about how she can fly as she writhes in her asylum constraints.

It's a betrayal, not just of Nancy and her feminism and her queerness, but also the genuine warmth and sensuality of adolescent female friendship that runs through the coven scenes.

* * *

Friendship didn't come especially easily to me. I did not go to all that many parties at school, but one does stand out. We had a Whodunnit role-play evening at someone's house, an oddly fuddy-duddy option for 16-year-old girls in retrospect. Anyway, we were each given a card. I was a married fund manager (not the murderer), and it turned out I was having an affair with an actor half my age (a role played by my best friend at the time).

About halfway through the evening, our affair was exposed. We had very much got into the swing of things by now and ended up staring into each other's eyes, her hand on my knee. And she made eye contact with me, a proper look of yearning.

The strange thing was we were not attracted to each other. And it was acting, of course. All the other girls giggled at the sight of this. But the intensity of it went on for a good beat longer than I would have expected. When the tension broke, we both laughed along with everything else.

The thing about female friendship for a bisexual girl was that it was a source of danger, but also of shelter, a safe space to explore attraction. *The Craft* nails that but also betrays it. I think that's why I never much feel the urge to watch it again, despite its importance to me.

At the end of the film, Bonnie and Rochelle come to see Sarah. They seem repentant, but it becomes swiftly apparent they are wheedling for their powers back. When Sarah bats them off, they conclude she must have lost hers too. Sarah whirls around on them. She makes the sky darken, and the wind blow hard. Lightning hits a nearby tree. Bonnie and Rochelle drop to the ground as a branch crashes down next to them, a final lesson.

"Be careful," Sarah says in her breathily didactic tones. "You don't want to end up like Nancy."

Perhaps. Take it from me, though; you don't want to end up like Sarah, either.

Author Bio

Anna holds an MA in Creative Writing from the University of East Anglia. Her short horror fiction has appeared in Mslexia, Ghost Orchid Press anthology 'Rewired: Divergent Perspectives in Horror,' Gothic Nature Journal, and The Crow's Quill. She is the winner of the #micropoem21 and 'Hot Poets' competitions. She lives in Croydon with her family and works in sustainability in education.

Go to @orridge_anna or @GreyElm@mastodon.online to discover more about her climate activism, writing, and love of all things corvid.

Reinventing Tropes
Mark Allan Gunnells

I love horror tropes. I've said it, and I'm not ashamed. I adore them all. Vampires, witches, werewolves, zombies, slashers with sharp knives, these were like candy to me growing up. In fact, if I had been given a choice between horror movies and candy, I might very well have chosen horror movies. That is how deep my devotion to the genre goes, starting at a very young age.

I should clarify that my journey into horror started at a most impressionable time in my life. I like to joke, though it is the truth, that I knew I loved horror before I knew I was gay. In fact, one of my earliest memories is of watching a horror movie with my family. The year was 1979. I was all of five years old, and my family sat down over two nights to watch the original airing of the *Salem's Lot* miniseries. My family was fairly permissive when it came to what I watched, and it never occurred to them that I shouldn't be watching as well.

I still remember specific scenes from that initial viewing. Yes, the Glick kid scratching at the window, which everyone seems to remember, but also Mrs. Glick waking up in the morgue and going after Ben, the vampire killing Mark's parents by conking their heads together, and that tragic, heartbreaking ending with Susan. These scenes imprinted on my young mind, but what lingers with me even forty years later was how the movie made me *feel*. It was exciting, frightening, suspenseful, and got a real reaction out of me.

The next horror movie I remember watching was *The Exorcist*. I was much more mature by that point. Ten years old! I have to confess that I didn't make it through that viewing. At about the midway point, I ran around and hid behind the sofa, prompting my mother to send me to bed. However, as frightened as I was by the film, from that moment on, I was hooked. I couldn't get enough horror.

If I had to analyze why, I think it is because while I had seen lots of different kinds of movies by the age of ten, none of them got the kind of emotional reaction from me that horror did. In fact, most of them I couldn't really remember by the time I was fifteen, but those horror movies remained as vivid as when I first watched them.

So, I started watching every horror movie I could. Some were cut-up versions aired on network TV, some I walked down to the local one-screen theater to see (back in the 80s when a child could buy a ticket for a rated R movie, and no one batted an eye), but when I was a teenager, we got our first VCR, and then it was nothing but a steady diet of horror. I raided the horror sections of every video store in my town, and what started as a love of cinematic frights soon enough turned literary.

Like most horror fans who came of age in the 80s, Stephen King was…well, King. And that led me to Clive Barker and Anne Rice, and that was a real game changer for me. More on that later.

I should say that while I was going along this horror journey, there was another more personal journey going on as well. I knew I was different from an early age, even before I could put words to that difference. I knew when I watched *The Dukes of Hazard,* for instance, I was much more interested in Bo and Luke and their tight jeans than Daisy in her short shorts. And starting in kindergarten, the other kids sensed my difference and promptly began to ridicule and torment me. I was too sensitive, and I didn't have an interest in sports or army men or any of the things in which boys were supposed to be interested. I listened to music and watched shows that were considered "girlie." I was even told that I carried my books like a girl, clutched against my chest as opposed to down by my side like a boy should.

In short, I was considered a sissy, a pansy. A fag.

By the time I was in junior high and puberty was in full swing, I knew I was gay. Oh, I fought against that knowledge and tried to change it. I went through a heavy religious period, but that's another story for another day.

In retrospect, I can see that my growing love of horror corresponded with my growing acceptance of myself and that the horror movies and books I consumed were providing me with something I found comforting and empowering as a gay person.

For one, the final girls in these movies were often the good girls, the bookish girls, the girls that didn't quite fit in. Laurie Strode in *Halloween* was insecure, interested in books and studies, awkward around boys. Hell, even her two best friends make fun of her. I could relate to this kind of character, and what really drew me in was that this character was the hero, the one we were meant to root for. That was the case in so many of the 80s horror movies.

And as perverse as it may sound, the victims in these movies usually seemed like all the bullies who tortured me daily at school. To be clear, I'm not saying I wanted these people dead, but there was a certain catharsis in seeing them fall while the person who felt more like me persevered. There seemed to be some powerful metaphor going on there.

And when I say the books of Barker and Rice changed the game for me, I refer to how they took traditional monsters and made them into the protagonists, the heroes. I knew society viewed gay people as monsters, as one-dimensional villains. Barker and Rice gave us the interior lives of these monsters and showed they were creatures of great sensitivity and power and worth. That was an invaluable lesson for me.

As I devoured more and more horror, I fell in love with the tropes, the traditional monsters and themes, and to this day, I continue to love those. What some call clichés, I call quintessential elements of the genre.

The only thing that bothered me growing up was that I rarely saw myself reflected in the genre I loved. If a gay character did appear, more often than not, it was a one-note character with little depth or authenticity. I think we all as people yearn for stories to act as mirrors so that we can find ourselves in the narratives. The horror genre in the 80s and into the 90s provided no such reflection of my own experiences. I had to put myself into the shoes of the final girl, but that was a compromising transmutation, and after a while, it became exhausting.

There was such a lack of representation, in fact, that when I first started writing horror fiction, I didn't utilize gay characters myself. I simply didn't think it could be done, not if you wanted to actually find a place at the table. I was erasing myself from the genre because I didn't think the genre would accept me.

A couple of things in the 90s began to change my mind on that subject. First, Barker publicly came out as a gay man and went on to write a long and complex horror/fantasy novel with a queer protagonist that touched on many gay themes, and this was published by a major New York house. Then I discovered the transgressive works of Poppy Z. Brite, a trans author who included queer characters in his work in a casual but very dynamic way. His characters were not queer in name only but had active and hot sex lives. These weren't the one-dimensional, asexual shadows I had been asked to settle for in the past, but complicated people with passions and personalities that truly brought them to life.

This started to give me the courage to bring queer characters into my stories. I had personally begun coming out of the closet; it was time I brought my work out of the closet as well. And during that crucial time in the mid-90s, my greatest abiding interest in horror was born. I grew up on horror tropes, and I loved them dearly. In my fiction, I wanted to explore those tropes in new ways, reexamining and reinterpreting them filtered through a queer lens. I felt I could breathe new life into these familiar scenarios by finally putting LGBT characters front and center. Even I was surprised by how fresh a trope could become when you saw it through the eyes of people the audience wasn't used to encountering in those kinds of stories.

I can still remember the very first story in which I had major queer characters. It was an eventually-abandoned vampire novel called *The Apprentice*. Not surprising it should be a vampire story because, at the time, I was obsessed with vampire stories. Inspired greatly by the works of Anne Rice and Poppy Z. Brite and Tanith Lee, I was a fang addict. Honestly, before *The Apprentice*, I had already written much vampire fiction, but this was the first time I let the characters be unapologetically queer, and they definitely had plenty of sex. What followed was a string of linked stories about an all-vampire rock-n-roll band called The Beasts of Burden. These tales were wild and sexual and uninhibited.

I liken it to when gay people initially start coming out. I don't know what it is like for young people now, but when I came of age, society as a whole was a frightening and dangerous place for queer people. There were no beloved gay characters on TV, and most thought AIDS was God's punishment for being queer. We were banned from the military, and marriage equality was so unthinkable it might as well have been science fiction. Therefore, most of us spent our formative years trying to suppress, trying to fit in, afraid to be honest about who we were and how we felt. When we reached a point where we decided to say fuck it and just be ourselves, it was an intoxicating kind of freedom. When you spend so much of your life afraid to tell people, when you finally get past that block, you want to tell *everybody* because you are so enamored of the fact that you are no longer afraid.

Therefore, some of my early work read almost like gay porn with a few horror trappings thrown in. As time passed, I began to tone the sexual aspect down, focusing more on crafting suspenseful and engaging tales of horror. However, I made sure to keep my queer characters sexual beings. I would continue to cast my stories with three-dimensional queer people, and I would continue to create stories that explored the familiar tropes of horror.

My third published book, which was my first significant work of queer horror, was a novella called *Asylum*. This was a zombie story that followed the traditional formula of a group of disparate survivors trapped together in a building while the dead tried to get inside. My new twist – the building in question was a gay nightclub, and almost all the characters were queer.

I came up with this concept because, at the time, I was watching all these Romero-esque zombie films and realizing that there were never any LGBT survivors. (This was before the age of *The Walking Dead* when we would get gay-in-name-only characters that never seemed to have the kind of dynamic romantic lives that every single straight character around them got to have.) I was actually watching the remake of *Dawn of the Dead* and got excited because there was a character I thought presented as gay, but then he ended up banging the hot blonde chick, and I actually said out loud to the screen, "Where are all the gay people? Do we not ever survive shit?"

In that exact moment, the idea for *Asylum* was born. A group of gay people from different walks of life, all with their own scars from growing up gay in a society that devalued them, trapped together, and tried to survive the night. I had so much fun working on this piece because I felt it was providing an exciting zombie story in a format people would recognize, but through the characters, I provided insights and personalities, and issues that you didn't see in the average zombie story of the time.

I won't lie; a few publishers passed on the novella before it found a home. Not all of them cited the queer aspect, but some were very upfront that they felt that the straight male audience they viewed as their potential buyers would be uncomfortable with a story full of gay characters and even some gay sex thrown in. I did not let that deter me. I kept sending it out, determined that if push came to shove, I would self-publish the thing.

Eventually, I found a publisher that embraced the story, did not balk at the queer aspect, and published it as a mainstream zombie release for general horror readers. To my delight, the book was well received and got some lovely reviews from those very straight male readers that some of the early publishers feared would never accept the work. The feedback I received suggested what they enjoyed most were the characters because that brought a new dynamic to a familiar story. The plot might have fit into what some considered a formula, but at that time, having gay characters that were more than jokes or shadows felt a bit revolutionary.

I don't pretend I was a one-man revolution. A movement was beginning with more queer creators providing queer representation in horror, but this was still the early days of the movement, and it was exciting to watch it begin to unfold.

The reception to *Asylum* cemented my passion for reinventing horror tropes by filtering them through a queer lens. I wanted to write stories about all the classic themes and monsters. I have tackled not only zombies and vampires, but ghosts and werewolves and witches and slashers and possessions. It's not like I'm just going down a list and checking off horror tropes, but it happens naturally because those are the tales I grew up loving, and I still remember how it felt to not see myself reflected in the stories that I loved. I want to make my work a mirror for queer readers today who have that same hunger for representation.

At this point, I do think it is a Revolution with a capital R. There are so many great queer horror writers working today. From Aaron Dries to Hailey Piper, Lee Thomas to Eric LaRocca, we are a force in the horror community, and I'm ecstatic to be a part of a movement for greater representation.

For my part, I will continue taking the classic tropes that first made me become a horror fan and putting queer characters into them. This may seem trivial to some, but as both a storyteller and a gay man, it is vitally important to me.

Author Bio

Mark Allan Gunnells loves to tell stories. He has since he was a kid, penning one-page tales that were Twilight Zone knockoffs. He likes to think he has gotten a little better since then. He loves reader feedback, and above all, he loves telling stories. He lives in Greer, SC, with his husband, Craig A. Metcalf.

Sordid Sapphics: The Demonization of Queer Women in Horror

E.E.W. Christman

"We always share a bed when we have slumber parties."

Jennifer smiles as she strokes Anita's hair. Their eyes lock. Her hands linger. She kisses Anita. Nervously, tentatively. Anita looks terrified but doesn't pull away. The opposite, in fact. She climbs on top of her former-best-friend-now-demon-succubus. They explore each other. Jennifer's hands slide up Anita's shirt. Her legs spread. Then, like a lightning strike, the moment passes. The spell over Anita fades, and she rolls away, screaming a frustrated *what the fuck is happening* at the ceiling.

And so ends the brief but poignant romance between Amanda Seyfried and Megan Fox's characters in the cult classic *Jennifer's Body*. Horror as a genre loves a sapphic romance…under the right circumstances, that is. But what are those circumstances, and what cultural significance do they carry? In the aforementioned movie, certain narrative conditions had to be met before the heroine and villainess could lock lips.

First and foremost, the film establishes Anita's "unhealthy" attachment to Jennifer. Her nickname is "Needy," as in she *needs* Jennifer's attention and validation. Her boyfriend Chip is suspicious–even jealous at times–of his girlfriend's obsession with Jennifer, declaring that Needy "always does what Jennifer tells her to do." He even tells Jennifer to "stop kidnapping his girlfriend," behavior that seems possessive at the beginning of the film but is quickly validated later on. This may seem like a small detail, but it has a long tradition in horror media. Women-centric relationships are often portrayed as inherently toxic, and more importantly, as dangerous. And That means the titular teen in *Jennifer's Body* can't just be problematic; she has to become something much worse. In the words of Needy herself, "Hell is a teenage girl." Jennifer had to transform from a kind-of-shitty bestie into an actual monster before the film would dare have a makeout session between its two main characters.

This begs the question: Why?

Horror relies on the myth of safety within the hegemony. A peaceful Midwestern suburb, a nuclear all-American family, living at the end of a quiet cul-de-sac, devastated by something invasive within their community. A perfect metaphor for anything that might threaten the status quo. In *Halloween*, it's a neurodivergent killer who escapes from an asylum; in *Dracula*, it's a lustful foreigner; and in *Jennifer's Body*, it's sapphic love.

Women-centric romance is inherently dangerous to hegemonic culture. It removes men from the equation of lovemaking. Sex is power, after all. And there is nothing more terrifying in a patriarchal culture than a woman who can't be controlled by men. We see this in the femme fatale trope. When a woman owns her sexuality, when she doesn't need nor want a man to protect her, she is automatically a villain. The heroines in such narratives are the opposite: they rely on their men.

In the noir thriller *Niagara*, Polly is the obedient wife who loves and supports her husband, whereas Rose is the scheming murderess trying to run away with her secret lover (never mind that Rose's husband is absolute trash). This is the classic virgin/whore dichotomy, where sexual purity is seen as pious, and sexual "deviancy" is seen as inherently evil. In horror, this is best represented in the "final girl," the one who survives the monster's assault and, usually, defeats said monster. In *Jennifer's Body*, Anita is sexually inexperienced and in a relationship with a man. She defeats Jennifer, her more overtly sexual friend. However, she doesn't come out the other side unscathed. Final girls rarely do. She's been "tainted" by her demonic bestie. That is the nature of horror, after all: a loss of innocence. You can't go back to the quiet cul-de-sac. You can't unkiss your friend. Her safety is shattered, in this case, by queer romance.

But *Jennifer's Body* isn't alone in this. It isn't even the first. There is a long tradition in film, especially horror, of demonizing sapphic relationships, going as far back as the Depression. In *Dracula's Daughter*, the 1936 sequel to Bela Lugosi's *Dracula*, Countess Marya Zaleska stalks the streets of London in search of prey under the ruse of looking for models. A woman comes back to her studio with her. The countess has her victim disrobe, watching her hungrily as she does so. Later, she kidnaps another woman and puts her in a sleep-like trance. Zaleska caresses her, then crouches over her sleeping form intimately just before attempting to feed on her. Again, this homoerotica can only be depicted as inherently dangerous in order to preserve the feelings of heteronormativity. Zaleska is a monster, using the other women in the film to fulfill her own desires. This was one of the first in a slew of vampire lesbian films, birthing a campy new genre, all with the same tropes: the vampiress lures women away to their doom. Like most lesbian/sapphic characters in horror, the countess seduces straight women. What she offers is temptation, and the price is your life. Queerness is lava, and heteronormativity is the sofa you must precariously stand on to avoid getting burned.

Homoeroticism is presented as being a seduction *away* from the norm in such films. The heroines are always attached to men–which are presented as healthy relationships in contrast to their gay counterparts–and are tricked or manipulated away from them. I can't think of a modern movie where this trope is more perfectly expressed than *The Moth Diaries,* which borrows heavily from the classic gothic novel *Carmilla.*

The film takes place in a girls' boarding school and watches as the protagonist, Becca, spirals, believing her best friend is being consumed by a vampire. Ernessa is the new girl in school, and the protagonist becomes jealous as her best friend, Lucy, starts hanging out with her. Where everyone else sees another girl, Becca sees a monster seducing her friend away from her. Becca's obsession with Lucy and Ernessa is immediately called out by everyone around her. After her father's suicide, Becca had no men in her life. She formed an unhealthy bond with Lucy, and Ernessa threatens that bond. Lucy and Ernessa become romantic partners, and when Becca finds out, things quickly devolve. Even her poetry teacher calls the girls' relationships "toxic." Quite an ironic claim since this adult man says this moments before kissing his teenage student. However, his claim seems to be supported by the narrative: without male attachments, women-centric relationships become burdensome and unhealthy.

As the film progresses, Lucy grows weaker and sickly. She rejects Becca entirely and only wants Ernessa. Again, the rhetoric reinforces the idea that the chaste love offered by Becca is good, and the sexual love offered by Ernessa is evil. In fact, Ernessa's affection is not only toxic, it's killing Lucy slowly. Rather than feeding on her blood like Countess Zaleska, Ernessa uses sex to drain her victim. And like Becca, Ernessa's father committed suicide. Both lack a strong male role model in their lives, the blueprint upon which they were supposed to build "healthy" heteronormative relationships. The protagonist relies on the friendship of other girls to fill this hole in her life, signifying her inherent "goodness," whereas Ernessa has chosen something more sexual, becoming monstrous.

Like the novel it is loosely adapted from, this obsession with relationships with other women is ultimately the downfall of all involved: Lucy slips away, Ernessa is burned, and Becca is taken in by the police. Just like *Jennifer's Body*, no one comes out the other side unscathed. They are all marked by queerness and punished for it by the narrative. As Needy says at the very beginning of the film: "I used to be normal."

Let's return to *Jennifer's Body*. In the film, Jennifer is chosen by an indie band as a virginal sacrifice in order to attain wealth and fame. The ceremony works. However, Jennifer isn't actually a virgin, so instead of perishing, she becomes permanently possessed by the demonic force. Her lack of innocence damns her, and she becomes a succubus, feeding on the boys in her small town. Eventually, she even devours Chip, her best friend's boyfriend. Her sexuality is directly linked to her "evilness" and her lack of remorse for this ultimate betrayal.

The movie is dubious about Jennifer's morals, to begin with, but after her transformation, there is no doubt about it: she's just *bad*. A literal maneater. Jennifer morphs into an uber femme fatale, only looking out for herself and using men (and women) to satisfy her own desires. Just like Ernessa and the countess, Jennifer's affection is dangerous, and becoming intimate with her has a hefty price tag: death. On the flipside, Needy is a standard final girl. Kind of vanilla, innocent enough to be sympathetic but not so innocent as to be boring. It's important to note that "innocence" in this context does not mean "sexless" (at least, not anymore). Needy does have sex in the film but in a safe, heteronormative context. According to the movie, Chip doesn't represent anything dangerous. Part of being "the good girl" means pleasing men; Needy *wants* to please Chip, in contrast to Jennifer, who uses her sexuality to get something for herself.

It's funny that so many of these films choose to vilify sex with women without even acknowledging the inherent danger men pose. In this way, *Jennifer's Body* differs, at least slightly. The indie band *Low Shoulder* invites Jennifer to join them in their van. She becomes terrified that they are going to sexually assault her. While the movie admits that men are dangerous to women, it does so while simultaneously slut shaming Jennifer. After all, she wouldn't be in this situation if she'd listened to Needy. If she'd been less interested in sex with strangers, she would've simply gone home. The movie ultimately places the blame on the band, with Needy hunting them down to get revenge, but not before it makes sure to point an accusing finger at Jennifer and say, "This is what happens to bad girls. And it could happen to you, too."

When Needy kills Jennifer, she obtains aspects of the curse, becoming demonic herself. The movie opens at the end of the plot, with Needy in a women's asylum. Before we even have the whole story, we see Needy being punished. Out of the gate, she is labeled as a problem. We know something is wrong with her. She's not normal, nor is she innocent. She is violent and mean, tempered by a trauma we haven't even witnessed yet. But the message is clear enough: this is a bad girl, and this is where bad girls go. Difficult women have to be punished, even heroines.

Becca in *The Moth Diaries* is similarly punished for her sapphic obsession; the end of the movie is her on her way to the police station, presumably to be arrested for setting fire to the school.

Both of these final girls are marked by their "toxic" relationships with women, one figuratively, the other literally. Needy bears a scar from her fight with Jennifer. Their final confrontation is in Jennifer's bed, weirdly reminiscent of the scene where they kiss. Needy on top of Jennifer, their eyes and hands locked, both grappling for dominance. One scene is intimate, the other is violent, but both are presented as threatening. In both, Needy loses an aspect of the purity that protects her from being punished by the narrative. In the first, she succumbs to sapphic lust. In the second, she is released from complacency and takes control, becoming violent. And although she is the hero, "good girls" aren't self-reliant. They are, in a word, needy.

They need protection, they need help, they need to be defended. So, Needy is caught and blamed for her friend's crimes. She saves the day, but at a price. She is a final girl, after all, and final girls never retain the rose-tinted glasses they had at the beginning of their stories. In *Jennifer's Body*, however, Needy becomes something between what she was and what Jennifer became. She is not a femme fatale, nor is she a final girl. She's something else. Still dangerous but also valiant. The film closes on her escaping the asylum. She hitches a ride to a Low Shoulder concert, claiming it "will be their last show."

Growing up queer, I always saw myself in these damsels of distress. I had a hard time relating to the fainting

Fay Wrays of cinema, or even the resourceful Jamie Lee Curtises. I wasn't a "good girl." Hell, I wasn't even a *girl*. But these otherworldly femme fatales, who defied so much of what was expected of them; how could I, a budding nonbinary femme who also liked kissing girls, *not* relate to them? Even as I write critically about the ways in which these tropes are problematic, I still adore these movies. Or, at the very least, parts of them.

I love powerful women. I love mean bitches who do whatever they want. And as a lifelong lover of horror, if they scare me, all the better. In the words of Brittney Slayes, "Nothing is scarier than a powerful woman." Isn't there something kind of amazing about seeing a woman *not* catering to the men in her life? Countess Zaleska is so powerful the movie couldn't even allow the protagonist to be the one to kill her. Ernessa doesn't meekly accept death, nor does she fear it. She straddles the line between life and undeath, answering to no one. After being murdered by men who were using her body, Jennifer flips the script and uses men's bodies.

And that is why these tropes persist and are so effective with mainstream audiences. These monstrous women represent a deviation from heteronormativity. They are beautiful, enticing, but also deadly. They *must* be deadly in order to vilify the alternative they offer. They threaten more than lives; they threaten the status quo. When straightness is the norm, queerness must be aberrancy. In this manner, queerness becomes a separate entity from humanity in these movies. It's more closely associated with the fiends than with living, breathing humans. And there lies the heart of the problem. When I saw these movies as a kid, yes, I felt drawn to the antagonists, the boogeymen in the closets (pun intended).

But the message was always the same: the things about myself that I saw reflected in those sordid sapphics made me sordid, too. These were problems to be fixed if I wanted to fit in. Like most LGBTQ+ youth I've met, I already had trouble with that. How devastating to learn that I was the monster my neighbors feared. I was the thing threatening the peaceful Midwestern suburb and the all-American family at the end of the quiet cul-de-sac. I was the devastation invading their communities.

"I am not normal."

But like Needy at the end of *Jennifer's Body*, "normal" is no longer desirable. While it is true that we can't go back to the cul-de-sac, why would we want to?

Author Bio

E.E.W. (Izzy) Christman has been a freelance writer and editor for more than a decade. They earned their Bachelor's in Creative Writing and their Master's in Creative Nonfiction from Ohio University, where they taught writing & rhetoric for two years. They moved back to the west coast where they were functionally a "starving artist" for several years, taking odd writing gigs where they could while slinging coffee to pay the bills. They worked as a technical writer, ghostwriter, analyst, proofreader, and content writer. It wasn't until Izzy started focusing on the kind of work they cared about that their side hustle started to grow into their primary job. They began teaching creative writing classes at Hugo House, volunteered as a First Reader for *Strange Horizons* magazine, and blogged for Seattle's Gay City, a nonprofit focused on public health. Their love of speculative fiction led Izzy back to school in 2021. They began attending the University of Washington to earn their Certificate in Editing, which they completed in June 2022.

Their love of the written word can be traced back to high school: they won the Young Appalachian Writer's Award in 2007 with their short fiction. Since then, Izzy's writing has appeared in a number of magazines, anthologies, and podcasts, including *The NoSleep Podcast*, *American Gothic Short Stories*, and *Unwinnable Magazine*. They are an active member of the Horror Writers Association.

When they're not working, Izzy likes sinking into a good fantasy novel, playing video games, and (of course) watching horror movies.

Books of Infected Blood: Tales of HIV/AIDS in Horror Media

Jonathan W. Thurston-Torres

Here's a six-word horror story for you: "I have HIV. My partner doesn't…"

Many readers of that will hear an implicit seventh word at the end: "yet." It's a reasonable assumption. Given some of the real-life horrors of our sex education methodologies, our media headlines, and our fear-focused rhetoric of "clean," "dirty," and "free," it makes sense that we associate having HIV with both a death sentence[1] and imminent contagion. I once had a roommate refuse to eat my cooking anymore because she was scared of contracting HIV. If I had to make a wager, I would say at least two-thirds of Americans would read the above six-word horror story and genuinely believe that being a sexually active, serodiscordant couple is temporary, that my HIV-negative partner would eventually get HIV from me if we are having sex, regardless of protection and regardless of the simple fact that I'm undetectable.

As a long-time lover of horror, I have been fascinated by the ways that the genre tends to respond to contemporary cultural anxieties, as many academic scholars have noted.[2] The giant monster films of the 50s respond to the fears of the bodily and environmental effects of the atomic bomb. The slashers of the 80s respond to the sexual freedoms of the younger generations and their

---

[1] See Leo Bersani's "Is the Rectum a Grave?" from 1987.

[2] A fundamental text here would be David J. Skal's *The Monster Show* (1993).

liberalism. Even recently, in the COVID pandemic, we've seen Zoom-based horror films! So, it is perhaps not surprising that throughout the last quarter of the 20th century and our first quarter of the 21st century, we have seen many STI-focused horror works.

When I watch these films or read these books, I hope—maybe a bit too "positively"—to see HIV turned into a monster without necessarily turning its owner into a monster. And over the years, there have certainly been diverse representations of the virus. Here, I want to explore some of the highlights over the years; think of this chapter perhaps as a survey of HIV in horror. Of course, it won't be comprehensive. I know I'm always discovering more works that dealt with HIV in the past! And sometimes, these works just gloss over STIs, like the random syphilis diagnosis in *Dressed to Kill* (1980). Often, the presentation of HIV is, for lack of a better phrase, quite fucked up. But, fucked up or not, I want to explore some of these tropes and point to hopeful new directions for HIV in horror media, especially as the virus relates to queerness.

A history of HIV horror would not be complete without at least mention of the films of David Cronenberg. In his first STI work, *Shivers* (1975), a phallic, fleshy parasite starts infecting the residents of a Montreal apartment complex. It makes them horny. And it makes them hungry. Cronenberg's follow-up was *Rabid* (1977), following a similar premise of a sexually-charged parasitic pandemic, this time with a phallic-clitoral stinger of a parasite. Then, in 1986, Cronenberg remade *The Fly,* focusing more on the bodily decay of Seth and the monstrous birth implied by his lover's nightmare after having sex with him in this form. While none of these films explicitly deal with HIV, *The Fly* sparked a number of discussions of HIV in body horror, with critics like Robin Wood and John Harkness debating the level of premonition in the earlier two works for the HIV epidemic to come in the following decade.[3]

Cronenberg's works around sex and disease tend to come in a package deal with violence and viewer disgust. Indeed, one could imagine these films being taught in a high school sex education program as a warning: if you have sex outside of marriage, this too could happen to you. His work is indeed body horror, turning the body into a site for anxiety, and likewise, it is a form of ecohorror. In Marisol Cortez's essay on "the ecohorror of intimacy" from *Fear and Nature* (2021), the body is framed as potential for ecohorror specifically because it reflects cultural anxieties around bodily functions and processes that are considered private and counter to what defines "civilized" social life. STIs certainly fall into that realm, and Cronenberg is heavily invested in this idea—that one's own sexual bodily fluids can be the locus of horror.

Cronenberg does this with an almost shaming tendency. He says with these films that there is already a kind of social monstrosity at play that leads the virus to spread. The virus in *Shivers* wouldn't have spread if the professor hadn't been having sex with the apartment "slut," after all. Cronenberg situates the discourse of sexual disease within the realm of conservative sexual morés. To have rampant sex is to already be unclean, he argues.

Well, I guess I'd be the first to die in a Cronenberg film!

---

[3] Ernest Mathijs does an excellent job summarizing the contemporary readings of STIs in Cronenberg's corpus. See Mathijs, "AIDS References."

Rather counterpoint to Cronenberg but still contemporary is probably my biggest idol and inspiration: Clive Barker. As an openly gay horror writer who lived through the AIDS epidemic and has been at least accused of having HIV by an ex, he comes at this dilemma with rather different stakes. While Barker is just as invested in the body as a site for horror, he takes a different stance on it. In the 1988 "Tearing Your Soul Apart," Barker even said, "I'm a little more pro the body than David [Cronenberg] is. David tends to be quite down on physicality, and finally, there is an argument that he's being repulsed by the flesh he's writing about, whereas I tend to be having a good time with it. 'Long Live the New Flesh' would be a cry that would come from both our lips." And indeed, if you read his mid-80s anthologies, the *Books of Blood,* you'll find stories of body horror that are often queer and very often erotic.

Of particular note are the stories "The Age of Desire," "The Life of Death," and "How Spoilers Bleed." In these three stories, the body becomes a vehicle for disease, and eroticism laces these stories in intricate ways. In "The Age of Desire," an experiment goes awry, turning a man's libido up by 1000% to a "burning" sensation, making him rape and murder without regard for morality. In "The Life of Death," a long-buried plague is unearthed by a curious woman and only gets spread afterward by her rapist at the end. And in "How Spoilers Bleed," an exploited South American culture curses the would-be mercenaries with gradual body decay. Even dust on the wind can slice their body to shreds.

Each of these stories reflects rather unique anxieties for someone living with HIV. What side effects could our medicine have? Will there be long-term effects? What is it like to have HIV and be vulnerable? How much can the medical system really protect us? Of course, some of these questions have changed implications over the decades. After all, our medicine today can keep us undetectable. I can be as healthy as anyone else now. I don't have to be hospitalized for my HIV. But...it makes me teary-eyed trying to imagine being a gay man in the mid-80s reading these stories and finding even that kind of erotic beauty in these works, something that would have been tough to find elsewhere, especially with HIV being as fatal as it was then.

One of Barker's more underrated works too is his dark fantasy novel *Sacrament* (1996). In this book, a gay wildlife photographer responds to his experience during the AIDS epidemic with a fascination of photographing animals on the brink of extinction. There are these elements of loneliness amid the Gothic tones. We get the sense as readers that the protagonist, Will, has survived a lot and is struggling to just find the will to carry on while honoring the past. As Barker has said in an interview about the book, "Where I found the book a place of real growth for me was in starting to analyse the feelings I have towards an actual world ... and getting past despair, which is part of being alive right now and saying goodbye to too many fine young people who have been taken by AIDS way before their time, and feeling powerless and angry about what is happening in the natural world, on the environmental level." At least in part, that's the kind of hope Barker creates for Will in *Sacrament.* Even in the horror landscape he's woven, Barker allows space for an epidemic survivor to find strength.

Of course, the 80s was a decade rich with other interesting HIV horror works!

In the 1986 film *City in Panic,* a psycho killer specifically targets gay men who have HIV/AIDS, and the film very much considers these victims genuine victims. The film says, as Daniel W. Kelly has noted, "targeting those suffering with AIDS is so not cool for society." The 1988 film *Graverobbers* has an odd subplot around the idea that sex with the town's zombies is inherently safe sex: "And best of all she's safe, it's safe sex now, because we can't get AIDS from dead people." And *Flesh-Eating Mothers* (1988) follows the Cronenbergian (yes, I'm making this a word) approach and associates adultery with transformative disease.

In the 90s, we start seeing more of that post-epidemic HIV horror discourse along the lines of *Sacrament.* The best example that comes to mind are two books by Jay B. Laws, a gay, HIV-positive man who lost his life to the virus in 1992.

His first book, *Steam,* deals with two men in a surrealist gay landscape full of bathhouses and HIV. The novel manages to empathize with the real-life fears around HIV and the deconstruction of queer identity at the tail end of the epidemic. His posthumous book, *The Unfinished,* has a few short stories, but the largest one deals with a man dying from HIV and his struggle with a miracle drug cocktail that has disturbing consequences. Both texts respond to emerging queer anxieties about HIV, the medical systems we once trusted, and the corruption of the spaces where we once felt liberated.

Thinking of HIV horror in the 90s, I can't help but think of the comedy horror film *Killer Condom* (1996). While the film is not really centered on HIV, it reflects a number of anxieties about sex, protection, barebacking culture, and risk-reward management in sexual dynamics in a fairly sex-positive way. As antiretroviral therapy was advancing, it perhaps makes sense that the condom could be seen as monstrous. It would certainly be an interesting film to be remade today in the world of PrEP and PEP.

Vampires also became further connected specifically with HIV. We had the 1992 novel by Dan Simmons, *Children of the Night,* a re-telling of *Dracula* that reads vampirism as a potential cure for AIDS, paralleling the supernatural, undead experience with the AIDS experience (though I would note the book partakes in straightwashing the AIDS narrative considerably). And at the start of the new century, Octavia Butler's final novel, *Fledgling* (2005), dealt with vampires in a sci-fi horror context, considering the sexual implications of the transferal of blood, leading many scholars, including Marty Fink, to call Butler's monsters "AIDS vampires."

Otherwise, HIV seems fairly absent from 00s horror. For many, it seemed a long-gone thing, a virus from the past. But in the 10s came a major revival of STI horror, especially around HIV. It started perhaps with the 2012 film *Thanatomorphose,* which followed the Cronenbergian (I should really trademark this) approach by connecting sexual violence with bodily decay. Building off the film's success came two major films: *Contracted* in 2013 and *It Follows* in 2014, both of which explore the ethical implications of spreading sexual disease.

Contracted deals with lesbian Samantha and her contracting of a zombifying disease after a drugged rape. This makes it one of the first lesbian-centered STI horror films, to my knowledge. The film speaks a lot to loss of identity (and specifically, loss of queer identity and belonging in queer spaces) through the virus, as well as the damage that happens to social, intimate, and familial relationships the virus causes. The film's 2015 sequel, perhaps, is a bit more problematic, focusing more on the Patient Zero mythos. In his undeniably important (but equally problematic) journalistic exposé *And the Band Played On* (1987), Randy Shilts focuses a lot of his documentation of the AIDS epidemic on Gaetan Dugas, the alleged Patient Zero of the virus in America. However, as many have attested today, the claim is dubious at best and, honestly, not important. As Todd Heywood said in an interview in *Blood Criminals* (2020), people are unfortunately fascinated by the "AIDS monster," the archetypal figure of the nefarious and intentional infector. Even personally, I can attest to the fact that one of the first questions people ask me when I disclose is if I know who gave it to me, as if they want to go to their 21st-century closets to grab medieval pitchforks and torches. I have always stood by Heywood's other words, that "it takes two to tango" and that all sex is inherently a risk. Anyway! *Contracted II* focuses on Riley's search for the progenitor of the zombie sexual virus, very much perpetuating the (again) problematic myth of the AIDS monster.

It Follows is another interesting take on HIV in horror, as it adds a number of ethical questions to the discourse. In this film, a monster, unfortunately named It, slowly stalks you until it rapes and kills you and can only be survived by passing it on to someone else through sexual intercourse. Upon your death, it will return to try to kill the previous person in the chain. So, you're faced with the immediate decision: do you let it take you and therefore go kill the person who had sex with you, or do you go out and have sex and give it to someone else? This is a rather sex-positive film. People aren't characterized as sluts here, and consent becomes a complex affair here. When Jay (she/her) gets it, the sex seems consensual. It is only *after* having sex that Hugh chloroforms her, ties her up, and, upon her waking, explains that she now has a monster that is chasing her. She refuses to have sex, trying to find ways to defeat the monster. Her friend Greg says he believes her but isn't too worried about it and is confident he can handle the stress and anxiety. So, they fuck. But it turns out he was a bit deceptive and didn't really believe Jay in the first place! The film is very invested in the idea of "informed" consent. What qualifies as informed when it comes to STIs? Where does the responsibility to inform lie? That is what is at stake at this film's core.

On top of these seminal films, there are several short horror films that explore STIs and HIV. The 2013 "I Wouldn't Wish the Eighties on Anyone!" deals with a young man's fear that he has caught HIV through his sexual acts in the 80s. "STDemon" (2015) involves another young man having his dick possessed by a demon. And "Undetectable" (2015) tries to capture the guilt of an HIV-positive undetectable man who had previously infected another lover (though I wouldn't recommend this film otherwise as it inaccurately portrays just about everything HIV-related).

In these works, both present and past, we see the response to some of these cultural anxieties about HIV. The risk of decay, ineffective medication, crumbling relationships, loneliness, ethical responsibilities, and killer condoms have been core to HIV discourse for a long time (okay, maybe not killer condoms...). The anxieties these works communicate are generally quite real, and they have had varying levels of effects throughout time.

I know it is essential to queer horror theory to read the figure of the monster as Other and to therefore read the monster as queer. We like to identify with Frankenstein's monster or with Dracula (as I'm sure many of the essays in this collection can attest). But the queer monster, as a theory, hits different when you have HIV. You feel like you're walking around with a secret, like people would see you like one of the infected in *Shivers* or *Contracted* if they knew. If they'd give you a wide berth in the grocery store or refuse to touch your cooking…

In many of these works, I can relate to the experiences. I wish I had read *Sacrament* when I was first diagnosed. I wish I had read Laws' books then. Instead, I grew up with the very Cronenbergian (okay, now I'm getting a quarter every time this word is used) outlook.[4] My Southern sex ed is largely responsible for that. In these works, I find a kind of elderly wisdom and comfort. I have heard from so many gay men who lived during the 70s and 80s but *didn't* get HIV on how I shouldn't talk so much about HIV, how it's not as big a deal today as it was back then, and how lucky I should consider myself that I'm living with the medicines we have now. And it's 100% true! I can't spread my HIV. The CDC has said it's not even a 0.001% chance. They've said it's just zero at this point. I could bareback a thousand men, and they'd never catch HIV from me. My lifespan is the same as yours. I'm healthy as a horse (just wish I was hung as one). But I wasn't prepared for the weekly suicide requests ("Go kill yourself"), death threats, and general harassment and bullying it would lead to. I wasn't prepared to be listed on a national HIV registry. I wasn't prepared to be considered a biohazard in most states, even if I'm undetectable.

---

[4] Dammit, the word already exists.

HIV still has its horrors. I see them every day. In 2012, Cecelia Bolden was stabbed to death by her husband after she found out she had HIV and disclosed it. In 2015, Todd Heywood was attacked, beaten, robbed, and almost murdered by two men who thought he deserved it for having HIV. That same year, HIV-undetectable prison inmate John Dorn was sentenced to 21 months of solitary confinement after having consensual sex with an inmate (who just got solitary for a week). In 2017, Georgia state representative Betty Price asked if we could permanently quarantine all people who test positive for HIV. Last month, I received three messages saying I should kill myself because of my status.

I've loved seeing the revival of STI horror, and I hope we get many more films and novels in the coming years. For people like me, they really can give us a sense of belonging and a chance for us to speak up and against some of the systems that are threatening to us. These works show the world that people like us still exist, that we are living and thriving, and that there are new anxieties around HIV we should be responding to. So, perhaps, just maybe, I should write a different six-word horror story, one that responds to some of these anxieties.

I have HIV. The world knows.

Author Bio

Dr. Jonathan W. Thurston-Torres is an instructor for Albion College in Michigan. They are also living with HIV and are an anti-stigma activist in the area. Their exposé on HIV in 21st century America, *Blood Criminals,* was nominated for a Lambda Literary Award, and they have also given a TEDx Talk on the subject. Their Twitter is @jthurstonmsu.

Bibliography

Barker, Clive. *Books of Blood.* Stealth Press, 2001.

———. "Clive Barker: Tearing Your Soul Apart," *Your Worst Fears Confirmed,* 1988. From "Sex and Sexuality." Available at clivebarker.info/sex.

———. "Coming Out No Horror for Barker," interview with Wilder Penfield III, *Toronto Sun,* 17 Aug. 1996. From "Clive on Sacrament." Available at clivebarker.info/sacramentbarker.

———. *Sacrament.* HarperCollins, 1996.

Bersani, Leo. "Is the Rectum a Grave?" *October* 43 (1987): 197-222.

Bouvier, Robert, director. *City in Panic.* Massacre Video, 1986. 1 hr., 25 min.

Butler, Octavia. *Fledgling.* Jane Langton, 2005.

Cortez, Marisol. "From the Bedroom to the Bathroom: Stephen King's Scatology and the Emergence of an Urban Environmental Gothic." In *Fear and Nature: Ecohorror Studies in the Anthropocene.* Edited by Christy Tidwell and Carter Soles. Penn State University Press, 2021. pp. 153-73.

Cronenberg, David, director. *The Fly.* 20th Century Fox, 1986. 1 hr., 36 min.

———. *Rabid.* Cinépix Film Properties and New World Pictures, 1977. 1 hr., 31 min.

———. *Shivers.* Cinépix Film Properties, 1975. 1 hr., 27 min.

Crotchet, Shawn. "STDemon." 2015. 29 min.

De Palma, Brian, director. *Dressed to Kill.* Filmways Pictures, 1980. 1 hr., 44 min.

England, Eric, director. *Contracted.* IFC Films, 2013. 1 hr., 24 min.

Falardeau, Éric, director. *Thanatomorphose.* Bounty Films, 2012. 1 hr., 40 min.

Fink, Marty. "AIDS Vampires: Reimagining Illness in Octavia Butler's *Fledgling.*" *Science Fiction Studies* 37.3 (2010): 416-32.

Forbes, Josh, director. *Contracted: Phase 2.* IFC Midnight, 2015. 1 hr., 18 min.

Ford, Craig, director. "I Wouldn't Wish the Eighties on Anyone." 2016. 19 min.

Kelly, Daniel W. "Homophobia panic over 80s slasher *City in Panic.*" *Boys, Bears & Scares.* 15 Oct. 2016.

Laws, Jay B. *Steam.* Alyson Publications, 1991.

———. *The Unfinished.* Alyson Publications, 1993.

Martin, James Aviles, director. *Flesh-Eating Mothers.* Panorama Entertainment, 1988. 1 hr., 29 min.

Mathijs, Ernest. "AIDS References in the Critical Reception of David Cronenberg: 'It May Not Be Such a Bad Disease after All.'" *Cinema Journal* 42.4 (2003): 29-45.

Mitchell, David Robert, director. *It Follows.* RADiUS-TWC, 2014. 1 hr., 40 min.

Petri, Armand. "Undetectable." Together Magic Films, 2015. 16 min.

Shilts, Randy. *And the Band Played On: Politics, People, and the AIDS Epidemic.* St. Martin's Press, 1987.

Simmons, Dan. *Children of the Night.* Warner Books, 1992.

Skal, David J. *The Monster Show: A Cultural History of Horror.* W. W. Norton, 1993.

Thurston, Jonathan. *Blood Criminals: Living with HIV in 21st Century America.* Weasel Press, 2019.

Walz, Martin, director. *Killer Condom.* Troma Entertainment, 1996. 1 hr., 47 min.

Weisman, Straw, director. *Graverobbers.* Films Around the World, 1988. 1 hr., 30 min.

Choosing Your Genre: Sentimentality and Horror in *Glen or Glenda*

Vincent Bec

Any which way you turn, whether it's IMBD, Google, Letterboxd, Wikipedia, Rotten Tomatoes, or other, horror is glaringly absent from the list of genres attributed to Ed Wood's 1953 film *Glen or Glenda*. Most commonly, it is labeled a drama but will also be characterized as a docudrama and exploitation film. So how did I manage to slide a slice of drama into a book about horror?

While horror is technically definable as a genre meant to create feelings of fear, dread, repulsion, and terror, any horror lover knows it's not always simple to determine which films are horror films (Literary Terms 2017). Movies such as *Picnic at Hanging Rock* (1975), *The Shape of Water* (2017), and *Silence of the Lambs* (1991) have all been fervently declared horror by some but denied the label by others. Horror is malleable and loose. Some films are horror movies because they make their audience jump, others because they keep their viewers up at night, and others are horror just because they have the right vibe. Perhaps horror's flexible, boundary-blurring nature is just another reason why it is the darling genre of many in the queer community.

The bulk of *Glen or Glenda* is written as a drama; however, Ed Wood chose to infuse the film with the language of horror by implanting it with three distinct hallmarks: the mad scientist, a dark and stormy night, and Bela Lugosi. All three of these horror figures were made popular by the horror films of the 1930s and would be just as recognizable as devices of the genre in 1953 as they are today.

Wood begins and ends *Glen or Glenda* with these elements of horror. The film opens with Lugosi reading in an armchair surrounded by curiosities. He closes his book and stares down the audience, stone-faced, before launching into a monologue about humanity and change. His monologue is punctuated with cuts to flashing lightning in a stormy sky. When we join Lugosi again, he is mixing liquids in test tubes and beakers. At the end of the film, we once again find him reading in his armchair, where he delivers the film's last lines. By beginning the film with scenes that instantly connect the audience to horror, Wood primes them to watch the rest of the film from a different viewpoint. He then periodically reminds the audience of this framework by sprinkling in horror-based scenes throughout the film. Finally, Wood chooses to end the film with a horror scene, indicating that he wanted to make sure the presence of horror is something people remember about *Glen or Glenda*. Horror is both the audiences' first impression of the film and their parting thought. Without bread on either side, lunch meat is just lunch meat. The filling of *Glen or Glenda* may be a drama film, but the horror that sandwiches it together transforms it into something new.

Whenever I write about *Glen or Glenda*, a part of me worries that readers will think I am blind to the film's faults. As can be expected, some of the film's claims about transgender people and gender nonconformity are outdated, and, unfortunately, misinformation about marginalized groups can be dangerous. *Glen or Glenda* pushes the narrative that transgenderism is a mental health issue caused by some defect in a child's upbringing. Glen is a crossdresser because his father didn't love him, and his mother favored his sister. Ann is transgender because, in childhood, she failed to make friends and was unsuccessful at masculine sports; therefore, she spent too much time at home helping her mother do women's work. Because of its focus on gender nonconformity as a mental health issue, *Glen or Glenda* also claims that the desire can be cured when the inciting childhood trauma is properly addressed. LGBTQ+ activists have worked for decades to change public beliefs that queerness is a mental illness, curable, and trauma-based. I do not begrudge anyone the condemnation of *Glen or Glenda* for its critical inaccuracies. However, for me, it will always overwhelmingly be a film of desperate compassion and interesting progressiveness.

Despite its reductive theories on the causes of gender nonconformity, *Glen or Glenda*'s opinions on the solution to issues gender nonconforming people face are surprisingly contemporary. The stories of crossdresser Glen and trans woman Ann are primarily narrated by a psychiatrist named Dr. Alton, who treated each. Dr. Alton recounts each story to Inspector Warren, who is seeking an understanding of gender nonconformity while working on the case of a trans woman who committed suicide after being repeatedly put in jail for wearing women's clothing. Dr. Alton frequently emphasizes that each case of gender nonconformity is different, and therefore each case requires a different solution to the patient's unhappiness with the gender identity societally imposed upon them. For some, a sex change is necessary for their happiness, while others would only feel worse after a sex change. The argument over whether or not an effort to transition is necessary to identify as transgender is still a hot-button issue. Furthermore, Dr. Alton separates the issues of gender identity and sexuality while recounting Glen's story. He tells the inspector that cross-dressing is not an indication that a man is gay. People can be both straight and gender non-conforming. The separation of queer gender identity and queer sexuality is something the LGBTQ+ community still struggles to have recognized. There continues to be a strongly held misconception that gender nonconformity is just a symptom or sign of gayness. One of the main purposes of Dr. Alton's commentary throughout *Glen or Glenda* is to urge Inspector Warren not to put gender non-conforming people into the one-size-fits-all box we often still see implemented by society today.

Glen or Glenda understood its audience, in part because it purposely lured in a certain demographic. The sentence "I changed my sex!" is prominently splayed across its poster, along with "What am I... male or female!" and "The strange case of a 'man' who changed his SEX!" "I changed my sex!" was also a working title for the film. Throughout *Glen or Glenda,* various characters react to a newspaper headline reading "WORLD SHOCKED BY SEX CHANGE." Some characters, such as Glen, react to this headline with empathy, but many characters see the headline as shocking. Similar to the newspaper headline within the film, *Glen or Glenda*'s poster and alternative titles draw in those who see gender nonconformity as a shocking spectacle to be leered and laughed at like a 19th-century freak show. This assumption that the film's audience is watching the film with callous judgment is evident in the scene where a man who likes to wear dresses and earrings while maintaining a masculine appearance is presented. Dr. Alton's narration accuses the audience of laughing at the man and chastises them for it.

Glen or Glenda is a persuasive argument for the acceptance of gender non-conforming people. Not only does it recognize its audience, but it also uses two important argumentative strategies: anticipating objections and making concessions. The first opposing viewpoint the film tackles is the opinion that gender nonconformity is unnatural and, therefore, against God's will. Early in the film, Dr. Alton compares people who oppose sex changes to those who oppose other progress in society, such as planes and automobiles. The audience hears the thoughts of a series of people, including "Airplanes, huh. Why it's against the creator's will. If the creator wanted us to fly, he'd've given us wings." Dr. Alton calls these beliefs silly.

The film then returns to the same series of thoughts but adds arguments against sex changes. "If the creator had wanted us to fly, he'd've given us wings. If the creator had meant us to roll around the countryside, we'd've been born with wheels. If the creator had meant us to be boys, we certainly would have been born boys. If the creator had meant us to be born girls, we certainly would have been born girls." Because the earlier arguments have been called foolish by Dr. Alton, the audience is now hesitant to align themselves with these people and their beliefs, including their beliefs about sex changes. *Glen or Glenda* also anticipates the assumption that gender nonconformity creates deviance and meets it head-on with Dr. Alton asserting that allowing a gender non-conforming person to continue, and advance, their preferred gender expression actually leads them to work, play and think better, as well as make them a more successful member of their community because they are happy.

Glen or Glenda concedes to the perceived ignorance of its audience by calling the want to change one's assigned gender identity or expression a "strange desire," but again and again, the film contradicts this perspective. The same line that calls gender nonconformity strange goes on to claim that taking away a person's ability to fulfill their desired gender expression would be the same as taking away someone's arm or leg. Arms and legs are considered normal, natural pieces of the human body. Therefore, to place gender nonconformity into the same category as arms and legs is to imply that it is an inborn piece of certain people's existence.

"We were not born with wings, we were not born with wheels, but in the modern world of today, it is an accepted fact that we must have them," Dr. Alton says. "So, we have corrected that which nature has not given. Strangely enough, nature has given us all these things. We just had to learn how to put nature's elements together for our use."

Dr. Alton's assertion that these accepted new technologies do come from the natural world insinuates that sex changes, too, are natural. *Glen or Glenda* also frequently suggests that sex changes are far more common than the audience might realize. In one scene, Dr. Alton mentions that sex changes have been performed hundreds of times, and in another, he implies that there are hundreds of thousands of gender non-conforming people in the world. Something so common can no longer be unusual.

One of the splendid peculiarities of *Glen or Glenda* is it doesn't rely on showcasing abuse in its pleas for compassion. While the film does feature some of the hardships gender-nonconforming people face, such as obtuse reactions to the sex change headline and the trans woman's suicide brought on by discrimination, it is filled with characters acting as positive behavior models. Instead of leaning into images of pain and suffering to create change in the audience by making them feel sorry for gender-nonconforming people, the film has characters of authority explain how they believe people should respond to gender nonconformity. Investigator Warren does not mock the trans woman in his case. He seems genuinely moved by her death, and he seeks to understand her motives. While he may be entering his conversation with Dr. Alton from a place of naivety, he does not criticize or belittle the characters in Dr. Alton's stories. His willingness to accept Dr. Alton's recommendations on how to prevent the deaths of gender non-conforming people, regardless of how comfortable he is with the solution, shows that Investigator Warren recognizes that if he is to be good at his job of protecting people, he must have empathy for all people. Dr. Alton is clear about the oppression gender-nonconforming people face. However, the stories he shares highlight how gender-nonconforming people can lead happy, successful lives when they are shown compassion and are allowed autonomy over their gender expression.

When Dr. Alton speaks about the difficulty of having to hear insensitive remarks in the workplace about gender nonconformity, the audience is given the example of a conversation between two factory workers. We hear one worker make deprecating comments on the sex change headline while another worker responds with an impassioned argument in support of the trans woman in the news story. In the end, the originally critical worker yields to the opinion of the supportive worker and finds compassion. In this conversation, audiences are given a model of how to stand up for gender-nonconforming people when met with animosity.

Glen's fiancé, Barbara, is another audience-accessible character. When she discovers Glen's crossdressing, she reacts with shock, confusion, and concern, which may not be the reaction we are trying to normalize today but would have been relatable to the film's original audience. Earlier in the film, one of Glen's friends, who is also a crossdresser, revealed that his wife had divorced him after learning his secret. Barbara decides not to leave Glen like the intolerant wife but does have the socially acceptable response at the time, which is to verbally discourage Glen's crossdressing by turning it into a burden they will have to overcome. However, despite Barbara's verbal denouncement of Glen's crossdressing, her actions tell a story of acceptance. When she reveals she will not leave Glen, she hands him her sweater, which he has been desperate to wear. This passage of the sweater seems less like an indication of future change in Glen's desire to crossdress and more like a symbol of affirming his identity. This concept is further reinforced when Glen and Barbara talk to Dr. Alton. Barbara asks what she should do if Glen never stops crossdressing. The doctor explains that it truly wouldn't matter to her if Glen continued crossdressing because Glen's happiness and her love for him are what is important. Glen and Barbara get a happy ending through the promise of acceptance instead of the promise of change.

Giving the audience positive behavior models toward gender nonconforming people is important because it is less demeaning for the queer community than using queer suffering. Using the suffering of marginalized groups to change behaviors toward them can be othering. Their suffering becomes a spectacle for the dominant culture; it may be a sad spectacle, but a spectacle, nonetheless. Using a suffering-only approach to seek empathy also allows those outside the group to maintain feelings of superiority. It leads to pity over understanding. Showing both members of respected positions and common people react to gender nonconforming people positively makes intolerant audience members the other. What is wrong with you if all these people can accept gender nonconformity, but you cannot? This tactic is especially relevant in *Glen or Glenda* because it is painted as a pseudo-documentary.

While I can list many reasons to find *Glen or Glenda* fascinating, there is only one thing that makes my heart truly feel connected to the film. It isn't the film's precarious position on the boundaries of horror nor its arguments for compassion towards gender non-conforming people. *Glen or Glenda* makes my heart ache and sing because of how deeply personal it feels. The film begins with a title card stating, "Many of the smaller parts are portrayed by persons who actually are, in real life, the character they portray on the screen." This statement is the core truth of the film. Despite the poster's eye-catching phrase, "I changed my sex!" the majority of the film's runtime is dedicated to the story of Glen, who has no desire to change his sex. The story of Ann, the trans woman, is told very quickly during a small pause in Glen's story between his fiancé's introduction to his crossdressing and their final appointment with Dr. Alton. Glen is played by Ed Wood, and the character and actor share many similarities. Ed Wood was also a crossdresser. Glen's fiancé was portrayed by Wood's real-life girlfriend, Dolores Fuller. Glen shares Wood's inescapable love of angora sweaters.

Even some of the film's flaws can be traced to Wood's own experiences. The film asserts that Glen is a crossdresser because his mother preferred a daughter and therefore encouraged his feminine gender expression. Ed Wood's eventual wife, Kathy O'Hara, claimed that Wood told her his mother dressed him in girl's clothing as a child (Grey 1994). Another dubious opinion in the film is the theory that gender nonconformity is caused by men's clothing being more uncomfortable than women's clothing. Fuller mentioned in an interview that this viewpoint was one personal to Wood, who loved soft, cuddly fabrics that he could not find in men's clothing (Mclellan 2011). Although Glen is the main vessel for Wood's life story, Wood's experiences leak into Ann's background as well. Before her transition, Ann served in the air force. During her military service, she carried a suitcase full of women's clothing with her for comfort, but she dreaded the thought of anyone discovering the suitcase's contents. Ed Wood served in the Marines and would later disclose that he feared injury more than death because he was afraid that a medic attending to an injury would notice the women's clothing under his uniform (Pontolillo 2017).

Self-inserts in movies, books, and other forms of art are far from uncommon. However, watching *Glen or Glenda* feels like such a special, authentic glimpse into a person's most private thoughts, feelings, hopes, and desires. Dolores Fuller did not know that Wood was a crossdresser until she saw him in drag for *Glen or Glenda*. He hid it from her for the first year of their relationship (Mclellan 2011). In addition to being the director, Ed Wood is the sole writer listed for *Glen or Glenda*. This means he wrote Barbara's response to Glen's secret and therefore wrote how Dolores responded to his own. As a big daydreamer, I have had many daytime fantasies of being my sincere self in which I craft people's perfectly positive, accepting reactions to the real me. Wood has captured for an audience his most guarded hopes and daydreams. He recognizes that his cross-dressing may be a shock for Fuller but ultimately desires her permission to love angora sweaters and for her love to be unconditional.

Ed Wood spent a lot of time and money constructing his elaborate coming out. Regardless of what one might believe about his filmmaking skills, I find it unlikely that he would haphazardly throw random elements into a project that required such radical vulnerability. There would be no change in the clarity or message of the film if it started with the suicide case and relied on only Dr. Alton's narration. The dark and stormy scenes of mad scientist Bela Lugosi are technically unnecessary. *Glen or Glenda* is Ed Wood's autobiography, and he wanted it to include horror, whether it made sense to the film or not, because just like so many details scattered throughout the film, horror is a piece of him, and perhaps he felt it was a piece of his queerness as well.

I'm a bit Norman Bates-esque when it comes to my gender and sexuality, aka repressed to the max. It is hard for me to be open about my identities. Maybe it's because I grew up in a time where almost every discovery of identity, personal crisis, or even many everyday actions were dismissed with "oh, they're—" or let's be real, usually "she's just doing that for attention," but I have a fear of people, both in and out of the LGBTQ+ community, thinking I'm lying about my queerness.

Just like Ed Wood can't suppress his crossdressing, I can't stop wanting to be known. I just want to skip to the part where I am out and accepted by friends, family, and others in the community without having to do the hard work of opening myself up to people. My family hates my love of horror. They make snide remarks about it all the time, yet I am not afraid to talk about it in front of them. There are many beloved horror classics I have not watched, but I don't worry about being called a fake fan by other horror lovers. When I'm anxiously attempting to converse with someone I don't know, horror is quickly brought up as a topic of conversation. The identity of "horror lover" is my safe space when it comes to how I define myself to others, and I find that this is very entangled with my desire, yet reluctance, to be out as queer.

Horror is queer. I am queer.

Maybe if I talk about horror enough, people will make the inference, especially if I focus on explicitly queer-coded villains and films. Have I mentioned my favorite monster is Leatherface or that I love *Seed of Chucky* (2004) enough times yet? I don't know if Ed Wood felt the same connection between queerness and horror that I and many others do, but it is clear that horror was his comfort, and he leaned on it when coming out just as I have leaned on it during the many years of my self-discovery.

Author Bio

Vincent Bec graduated from North Carolina State University with degrees in Psychology, Media Communication, and Gender Studies. They write about how gender and sexuality are represented in film for both academic and non-academic platforms, including the feminist film magazine *Grim*. Their main focus is on the analysis of horror films.

Work Cited

Grey, Rudolph (1994). Nightmare of Ecstasy: The Life and Art of Edward D. Wood Jr. Feral House.

"Horror: Definition and Examples." *Literary Terms*, 16 Sept. 2017, literaryterms.net/horror/.

Mclellan, Dennis. "Dolores Fuller Dies at 88; Actress Dated Director Ed Wood." *Los Angeles Times*, Los Angeles Times, 11 May 2011, www.latimes.com/local/obituaries/la-xpm-2011-may-11-la-me-dolores-fuller-20110511-story.html.

Pontolillo, James (2017). *The Unknown War of Edward D. Wood, Jr.: 1942 - 1946*. Self-published.

Gothic Queer, Edward Gorey and Me
Catherine Lundoff

I had a haunted childhood filled with the ghosts of deceased relatives hovering just out of sight. My sight, anyway. Most of the time. My grandmother could see them quite clearly and interacted with them a lot. I quickly learned that talking about what went on when I stayed at her house at my elementary school or to other people elsewhere made me even more of an outcast than my stunted social skills. I may have also learned that talking to dead people was its own skill set…but I talked about that even less.

All that alone time left me bouncing around in my baby queer head, just me and all the books I could get my hands on. We didn't have a TV, so I read constantly in an effort to escape and tune out my surroundings, to find new friends in stories, to imagine new possibilities, and all the other reasons avid readers turn into avid readers (and sometimes, writers). As a result, my mother and a lot of her friends gave me books as gifts.

Amongst them were some of the early works of one Edward Gorey. Gorey (1925-2000) was an American artist, writer and costume and set designer who was born in the Midwest and transplanted to the East Coast in 1946 to attend Harvard. He moved to NYC in 1953 and began working in publishing as a cover artist and illustrator. A measure of fame and success followed, and he began creating independent artwork, books, doing set and costume design for plays and other performances, and eventually, the title illustrations for the PBS series *Mystery!*. He went on to develop a cult following drawn to his style as well to the content of his work and, as a result, a degree of commercial success that enabled him to buy a house on Cape Cod and support himself as an artist and writer.

Either Mom or one of her friends gave me one of his books when I was about eleven, which would have made it 1974. It was probably *The Gashlycrumb Tinies* because, from an adult perspective, any artwork or stories involving children must be geared toward an audience *of* children. Welcome to the late 1970s! I was also a morbid, withdrawn kind of kid, reading habits aside. So, dying children, murdered children, children vanishing into mysterious bogs, children being neglected and forced into child labor, all the horrors the imagination could conjure from a haunted childhood like mine were displayed in lovely black and white line drawings by an "eccentric" artist who lived in the same city I did. His stories made perfect sense to me, and that was a revelation.

It was as if I had acquired an uncle I never knew that I had, one that really understood the nightmare pockets of my brain. From an adult perspective, I can recognize that the not very thinly veiled queer content of his work for a grown-up audience, the "lady who likes other ladies" and the effete men clearly interested in each other more than anything else, probably didn't hurt. At the time, I understood them as outcasts and odd, but also as kin of some kind. Also, there were cats and opera divas and ballet and books, lots of books. How could the sort of child that I was resist getting pulled in?

In 1978, I leveled up my Gorey fandom. My mother took me to a production of *Dracula* on Broadway with Frank Langella in the title role. He was terrific (and smoking hot, even to my teenage not-yet-out as bisexual libido). But along with the barely restrained sexuality and sensuality of the play (and there was a LOT), the other thing that stood out was Gorey's sets. I adored the lovely, felted bats with their glowing red eyes that decorated the curtains. I shivered at the black/white blood-red palate with its illustrated spiderwebs and ruins. Here was decadence and decay, madness and terror and wonder, simmering sexual tension, and more. I had come home.

After a childhood spent with ghosts, a monster you could see and fight (or succumb to) was a miraculous new thing. I loved how both the story and the sets made the implicit terrors real and concrete. Of course, a vampire would live like this. Of course, a bookish kid who felt disconnected from the world around her would be able to relate to that feeling of isolation and a life lived well outside the ordinary.

I often think of this production as my first introduction to horror, and Gothic horror, at that, but in reality, I think it was a more gradual process and that this was just the standout event that stuck in my memory. I had seen movies and read stories about human and inhuman monsters before, but this play, with its sets filled with dark archways and corners and glowing-eyed bats, was something more. It still sticks in my imagination as a three-dimensional display of my teenage id.

I set off on a quest to find more things that reminded me of Gorey's work and made me feel the same way, which in turn sent me down the reading rabbit hole of Gothic romance, a genre that was readily available to me at my local library. Victoria Holt, Mary Stewart, and company took me on journeys with their imperiled heroines and their saturnine heroes with their dark manor houses filled with foreboding and many secrets. I read the Brontes'

Wuthering Heights and *Jane Eyre* as school assignments, which of course, meant that I gave neither their proper due, but Jane Austen's *Northanger Abbey* was a gateway into more nineteenth-century Gothic tales, and I enjoyed quite a few of those.

Is Gorey's work "horror," strictly speaking, his work on *Dracula* aside? I would argue most emphatically it is and much in the spirit of Gothic horror. Even though he generally used characters in Edwardian dress and style, the architecture of his settings, his style, and sensibility were very much influenced by Gothic art and fiction. What makes his stories horrible and captivating? *The Dwindling Party* has a family consumed by a mysterious garden, while *The Gashlycrumb Tinies* has small children dying in various horrible ways by way of teaching the alphabet. *The Loathsome Couple, Neglected Murderesses* (released in one book with *Dancing Cats*), and *The Deranged Cousins* all revel in murder and madness. Then there are the ghosts, the hauntings, the insect gods, the disappearing ballerina who may have become a giant bat and more, all squarely over the dark fantastic line into the horrific.

Did I read all of this as a teenager? No. Some of his more explicitly queer work, like *The Curious Sofa*, with its queer couples and triads and adventurous souls whose romantic and sexual adventures come to a ghastly end (off stage) when they are introduced to a very special piece of furniture, I didn't read until I was in college. Some of his other stories had elements I just didn't get until I came out after college. I know, I know, one is supposed to come out at college, not shortly thereafter, but so it goes. I will note that every room I had in every dorm or apartment that I lived in included at least one Gorey illustration, generally a signed poster of the unfortunate Charlotte Sophia, whose eyesight had begun to fail from making paper flowers by candlelight. The years before you figure yourself out can often feel like you can't see clearly that some disaster waits around every corner (like the motor carriage that kills Charlotte Sophia) and that you are utterly, terribly alone, like *The Little Princess* in reverse. Gorey's art and fiction continued to work splendidly as a metaphor for my life.

Did I consciously recognize Gorey as a fellow traveler in queerness? Well, there were, as they say, some signs. I came out as bisexual in 1986, and the number of straight cis men who rocked looks that featured rings on all their fingers, elaborate necklaces, and full-length fur coats and who obsessed about cats and ballet was vanishingly small (still is). And once you start viewing his work through a queer lens, it becomes increasingly difficult *not* to see it. The older gentlemen with their handsome young male companions, the ladies exchanging significant glances, all of these stand out when you look at them as a queer fan of his work. There is so much subtext that it's hard to imagine how anyone could have ever ignored it.

I should note that Gorey did come out in a couple of interviews. The thing was that he came out differently at different times. He and his roommate, acclaimed gay poet Frank O'Hara, created their own queer salon at Harvard in the 1940s. Were they lovers? Quite possibly. But in late 1940s American terms, they were "roommates." By 1980, he answered a question about his sexual orientation with "I don't know" and "I suppose I'm gay, but I don't really identify with it much." At various times, he was described as gay, bi, and asexual, which might have been labels placed upon him by biographers or ways that he identified himself over the course of his life. It doesn't make his work less queer, of course, but it makes the man himself more difficult to pin a badge on, which was exactly how he liked it, as far as I can tell.

I took a different path, coming out as I did at the height of what is now known as the "AIDS Era." President Reagan and his administration had only just begun to reluctantly acknowledge the disease as a public health crisis. Same-sex marriage, laws against discrimination, positive portrayals of queer people in mainstream media: these things were all pretty much nonexistent. The feeling that you needed to "pick a side" was very strong and perceived by many activists as necessary for our communities to survive. So naturally, I embraced a completely different kind of label and came out as bisexual/queer, which was seen at the time as a liminal status, one that wasn't a part of the "gay and lesbian community" for more than a few folks.

In that way, too, I felt closer to both Gorey and his work as something out of time, liminal, and boundary-crossing. Horror and fantasy and art and writing and macabre charm, all overlaid with queer sensibility and themes: reading and looking at his work brought me comfort long before I grew to appreciate it from the perspective of a writer as well. Whether I wanted an escape or a visit to another, weirder world, his books were a helpful anchor in my more turbulent years.

One of the other things that stand out for me in Gorey's work is his love of wordplay. Illustrations based on unusual words, as well as stories that consist entirely of words well outside common usage, fill his books. And, of course, there are the various alphabet books. While I cannot say that he inspired me to become a writer, he certainly did more for my vocabulary than some of my English classes.

Despite all that obvious inspiration, I did not start writing fiction until I was in my mid-thirties. Once again, I found myself viewing Gorey's work from yet another perspective. *The Unstrung Harp or Mr. Earbrass Writes a Novel* is a glorious bit of fun mocking both the writing process and the "unspeakable horrors of the literary life." It is one of the various short books where Gorey explored the burden of creativity for writers, artists, ballerinas, and opera divas. Sometimes, they vanish, like the mystery (and mysterious) author at the heart of the *Awdrey-Gore Legacy*. Or vanish offstage on a previously unplanned trip abroad. Or, well, are murdered since that is always a thing that happens in Gorey.

It was, I think, part of his perception that art and writing consume the artist, leaving nothing but a few postcards or the memory of gilded bat wings in their wake. I sometimes wonder if he thought he would just disappear one day, leaving nothing but a gilded bat costume or an empty chair sitting next to a pond behind. It is clear from his stories that he understood both the big highs and the big lows of the creative cycle for the professional artist. His ballerinas, for instance, find that fame and fortune bring opportunity (and peril), but it is also a lot of work, and their daily lives are often dull. Mr. Earbrass does a wonderful job at capturing this as well. By the time he has finished writing his manuscript, he never wants to see it again, let alone do revisions. Even dropping it off at his publisher's seems a bit too much. But he does it anyway because he must.

This, too, I think, is an area in which Gorey's work captures a quiet kind of horror, one that is far creepier than his child murderers and poisoners. Characters take aimless journeys, full of implied peril, but in the end, find nothing.

They leave the familiar behind, trading it, in some cases, for an absence, a disappearance from the heart of their own work. They are erased, and all that did, sometimes even the murders, vanishes with them. The reader can use the postcards of the *Awdrey-Gore Legacy* to assemble their own mystery, complete with a full cast of characters, a detective, potential victims and settings, but the author herself is only depicted in a card showing the empty chair where she was last seen.

Is Edward Gorey still a huge part of my life? Well, the last vacation we took pre-pandemic was a trip to Cape Cod to visit The Edward Gorey House in Yarmouth, MA. There you can admire the books and art, his fur coat, his jewelry, the latest generation of cats who are supported by his trust, and of course, a rotating series of themed art exhibits. You can buy prints with his embossed signature and walk through the garden admiring sculptures inspired by his work. The nearby antiquarian bookstore sells his memorabilia and books, and his legacy can be found in both the town and the surrounding area. Ghastly, odd, grim, hilarious and indisputably queer, Edward Gorey lives on, his legacy assured.

And me? I have a collection of his work on the walls and a collection of his books on the shelf. I even have the *Dracula* toy theater and a plethora of biographies, puzzles, and the like. I even sleep under a couple of his prints. He has become such a huge part of my life that I can't imagine it without him. Did Edward Gorey make me a queer horror writer? I like to think so. Tip of the morbidly inspired pen to you, sir, and thanks for all the weird.

Author Bio

Catherine Lundoff is an award-winning writer, editor and publisher. She is a recipient of a 2021 Ladies of Horror Fiction Writing Grant and was the Author Guest of Honor at Marscon 2022. Her books include *Silver Moon, Blood Moon, Out of This World* and *Unfinished Business* and, as editor, *Scourge of the Seas of Time (and Space)*. Her short stories and essays have appeared in such venues as *Queer Weird Western Stories*, *Divergent Terror*, *Sherlock Holmes and the Occult Detectives, Fireside Magazine*, *Nightmare Magazine*, the *SFWA Blog*, and several World of Darkness anthologies and games. She is the publisher at Queen of Swords Press and teaches writing and publishing classes at the Loft Literary Center, the Rambo Academy, and Clarion West Online. Websites: www.catherinelundoff.net and www.queenofswordspress. com

The Ghost of an Ordinary Man: *The Phantom of the Opera* on Heterosexual Marriage and Gender

Finley Lockhart-Willow

"Now I want to live like everybody else. I want to have a wife like everybody else and to take her out on Sundays. I have invented a mask that makes me look like anybody. People will not even turn round in the streets. You will be the happiest of women. And we will sing, all by ourselves, till we swoon away with delight. You are crying! You are afraid of me! And yet I am not really wicked. Love me and you shall see! All I wanted was to be loved for myself. If you loved me I should be as gentle as a lamb; and you could do anything with me that you pleased."

— Gaston Leroux, *The Phantom of the Opera*

Who is the Phantom of the Opera, and why is he so scary?

These are the two central questions posed by Gaston Leroux in his titular novel. He answers the way your mom might finally, reluctantly tell you why your childhood bully was like that, now that you're old enough to understand.

Straddling the lines between detective fiction, Gothic horror, and Gothic romance, *The Phantom of the Opera* is a fundamentally liminal work. It's subtly, insidiously terrifying, taking the image of a guardian angel and planting the seed in your mind that not only might the angel be a mere human man, but he might also be a flawed, irrational, violent human man who's dangerous to love and impossible to trust.

Joel Schumacher's 2004 film *The Phantom of the Opera*, on the other hand, is by no means a horror movie. That would come later. For now, I was eight years old and being (perhaps irresponsibly) shown the most accessible and digestible version of the story by my music teacher, along with a class of other impressionable kids.

None of the sexually charged scenes were commented on, and I'm sure they went fully over my head, but I distinctly remember being told: *I'll pause before he shows his face. You can leave if you don't want to see it.*

I didn't leave, and I was disappointed. All the common criticisms of Gerard Butler's makeup are true. He looks like a burn victim that healed miraculously well. He looks like he got stung by a bee. He looks like he's got a moderately bad food allergy. It's truly not that bad or scary in the slightest.

I wasn't horrified - I'd seen *The Golden Voyage of Sinbad*, after all. I could handle some mild to moderate scarring at age eight. My reaction was not the norm, though. Plenty of the other children left, and many of those who didn't leave covered their eyes and recoiled in horror when they peeked through their fingers.

What's wrong with him?

The movie gave them this answer: *A mean guy beat him up and put him in a freakshow when he was little, and now he's evil. That's what's wrong with him.* I was fascinated, I was sympathetic, I was intrigued, but I wasn't afraid.

Then I read the *novel*. And, needing hit after hit, I sought out the Lon Chaney film - certainly horror. And then the Claude Rains film. And then the Robert Englund film. And then *Song at Midnight*, claimed as China's first-ever horror film. The sad, sexy Opera Ghost that I'd first met as Gerard Butler had revealed himself to be a horror villain, and I was hooked.

Erik's kidnapping, his stalking, the echoes of past torture and assassinations, the murders, the extortion, all those things were just melodrama to me. Classic Gothic horror tropes that I was all too familiar with. Not frightening.

But something about his despair was chilling, almost prophetic: a glimpse into the life I'd be offered when I decided to transition in the future, the life I'd be expected to seek as a man if I wanted "normal" men - cis men - to view me as one of their own.

I watched *The Phantom of the Opera* performed on Broadway once, and I was left gutted and horrified by one sequence in particular: *The Point of no Return*.

Erik has written an opera for Christine to perform. It portrays him as Don Juan Triumphant, the epitome of male seduction. He is winning over *his woman*. He's going to become an ordinary man, a title that can only be achieved if he convinces her to be his wife. At least, that's what he thinks he wants.

And then, he steps on stage.

She leans into the music. Furious that he won't accept her love unless it's romantic, she takes an aggressive role, seeming to pursue him.

Fine, I'll give you what you say you want.

If he were truly the person he's pretending to be, he would be able to match her energy, to face her down as an equally forward opponent. Instead, he cringes back, he wavers, he looks like he wants to run. He is draped in shapeless black cloth, ostensibly to hide the fact that he's killed her previous costar and taken the man's place, but it becomes apparent that Erik, as he truly is, would not have been able to play this role, necessitating the disguise.

It's not like any of Erik's previous disguises. It's not the elaborate, ostentatious Red Death costume, accentuating his noseless skull-face with a carefully sculpted mask that turns his ugliness into a work of art. It's not a calculated flash of his disfigurement amid fine, gentlemanly clothing, meant to shock the ballerinas and feed the supernatural rumors he's begun to take pride in, even as he's desperate to escape them.

It's a complete rejection of Erik's personhood in favor of becoming the specter of the ordinary man. He's fully obscured, overwhelmed, and uncertain, no longer running the show, taking no joy in this costume that has been his only goal for so long.

This is not what Erik wanted. This is not who Erik *is*. And now he can't leave, not in front of all these people. He has destroyed his comparatively comfortable life as the Palais Garnier's charming local monster, killed too many people, and ruined too many lives, and he can't go back now. He has to keep playing Don Juan.

Erik is not an ordinary man, and the person he thought would be able to make him one is not an ordinary woman. She, too, has failed at heterosexuality and, thus, at gender itself. She loves her childhood friend Raoul even though society would never approve of an orphaned woman who works for a living marrying a nobleman like him. She tells

Raoul they can just play at being engaged, as if they're children again, playing make-believe - fully aware of the adult circumstances that make their desires so hard to realize but unwilling to prioritize them above the truth of her own feelings.

When Christine was cast as the page boy-a male character who's romanced by the female lead - instead of the lead role in an earlier production, it was against Erik's wishes. He has been training her, after all, and he knows what she needs to become - the leading lady. Christine herself is never asked if she truly prefers the traditionally feminine role. Likewise, when she is asked to become Erik's wife, to elevate the two of them to the magical status of a normal couple, it isn't truly a request - it's part of a contrived story for which he has quite literally written her lines.

She wants Erik to be her mentor, her friend, her Angel of Music - modes of affection that exist for their own sake, not as stepping stones on the road to heterosexual marriage - and this is something Erik can't accept.

It's not enough to be a man in his own way. He has to be like everybody else, and Christine, having doomed herself by loving him in a way unique to her - in a way that fails to make either him or her ordinary - has to be the catalyst for his metamorphosis, *or else*. One can almost imagine Erik saying: "What did she *think* was going to happen when she sang for me?"

The Opera Ghost, that flashy villainous persona full of panache and witty one-liners and spooky magic tricks, always has been and remains a source of gender envy. But Erik, the man who sacrificed the Opera Ghost to the cult of cis/hetero normativity, became a source of gender foreboding, a ritual scapegoat who served to help me exorcise my demons and show me what I should avoid on the road to transition.

For all that he embodies, certain aspects of misogyny, Erik is also treated as a madwoman by the narrative, and he spends all his energy trying to escape that, as if he's aware of the trope he's been assigned. He's hysterical, he's insane, he's emotionally volatile and obsessed with his appearance. He is fragile to the core and makes up for it with flamboyant displays of force.

Ultimately, he is isolated because he is ugly and mad, neither of which he can control, and both of which are relatable to me, having grown up both neurodivergent and viewed as a girl. Erik believes that life isn't worth living unless he's aesthetically pleasing, entertaining to be around, and desirable, and in a sense, he's right. The life he thinks he wants would not be worth living because other people would not allow it. He has crossed the border from "a man who can be ugly and volatile and still respected, because he's a man," into "someone who doesn't get to be a man, or respected at all, because of their ugliness and their madness."

Perhaps he's crossed that border, or perhaps he was born on the wrong side of it. He doesn't know why male privilege doesn't apply to him, only that, according to those he views as more fully human, his life will only be worth living once it does. He is never presented with the option of being a man, simply and uniquely, without the "ordinary" part.

To be removed from gender and placed into the category of "monster" must have been a more complex trauma than Joel Schumacher made it out to be. Erik was not simply beaten for being ugly. He was taught that, in order for him to have a life at all, his life must revolve around how fundamentally different he was from everyone else. It's no wonder that his self-made persona is a supernatural being - an angel, a ghost, a phantom - variously something more than human and something less, depending on how he feels about himself, but never quite human.

Erik exists in seclusion, and interactions with him are not viewed as *human* interactions. It's an encounter with the Opera Ghost; it's a visitation from the Angel of Music. Having been taught by his upbringing that nobody is willing to humanize him, Erik tries to give up being human, but he fails spectacularly, and his failure brings with it a body count.

The inhabitants of the Palais Garnier view him as an entertaining specter, but when he begins messily trying to enter the world of the living, they come to view him instead as a madwoman in their attic who must be put out of her misery to save them all a headache.

As with all fictional madwomen in all fictional attics, Erik is genuinely violent and genuinely dangerous. They're justified, of course, in putting him down, because he's hurting people.

In *Jane Eyre*, an earlier Gothic novel that shares the stock trait of having a "normal" love interest, a strange, frightening love interest, and a young woman torn between the two, there is a literal madwoman in the attic - the secret wife of the strange love interest, Mr. Rochester - his deep personal shame personified. However kind he wishes he could be to her, she is far too mad to continue living in the story she's part of, and she dies accidentally, but as a necessary part of the narrative.

Though Erik seems on the surface to be this story's Mr. Rochester, a problematic yet alluring older man with disturbing secrets, he functionally bears more in common with Rochester's wife, Bertha, and he shares her fate. However much the reader is meant to pity him, he simply cannot be allowed to live. In the novel, he dies of unspecified natural causes and heartbreak after being forced back into seclusion, with the implication that he died in spirit when he lost Christine, and in many other adaptations, he is killed by an angry, vengeful mob.

For all that his violence is horrific and unjustified (and it is *very* horrific and *very* unjustified), Erik is correct about one thing: He's been denied the chance to live as an ordinary man. The body that he was born with, exacerbated by a brutal life of exploitation that he never chose, does not allow him to live quietly, to be an eccentric but respectable artist in a nice little apartment going about his days in peace.

There's only one mark of ordinariness, of "true" manhood, that he feels he can access, and that's *having a wife*. There's only one woman he's close enough to for that to even be a thought in his mind, and unfortunately for her, that woman is Christine.

In loving Christine, in attempting to pursue the role of the Ordinary Man through her, he ultimately pulls her down with him into the role of the madwoman, putting her in an unbelievable and life-threatening situation. In his despair and isolation, he subjects another vulnerable person to despair and isolation, because he feels so deeply that he *has* to in order to become ordinary - and that, to him, is more important than being kind or being himself.

My relationship with this character, as a trans man who doesn't conform to masculinity or femininity, is complex and, at times, uncomfortable. It's not a perfect parallel, but the imperfections of the analogy make it something I can enjoy, whereas if it were more exact or less melodramatic, I might not be able to stomach it.

I'm the type of trans man who's often ostracized by other trans men, those who think that striving to pass perfectly at all times is the only legitimate way for us to exist. Before I went on testosterone, and when I was in the earliest stages of it, I certainly looked and sounded like what online trans culture terms an "Aiden": a soft prettyboy who doesn't make an effort to pass as a cis man and still insists on being acknowledged as male. Flower crowns, dyed green hair, short velvet skater skirts, multiple sets of pronouns, et cetera. It made some people ridiculously uncomfortable, but I had struggled so hard to reach a place where I could safely be myself that I wasn't willing to water it down at all.

Additionally, as an autistic person whose autism is usually visible to others, existing in the realm of gender and sexuality is often a struggle. I didn't start out from the position of someone who's expected to think about such things - I embarked on this journey having been preemptively degendered and rendered sexless in the eyes of society, a failed girl who would never truly become a woman, let alone anything else.

The Phantom of the Opera in all its forms was the first place where I truly felt like I saw myself - variously in Erik and Christine, in his failure to be viewed as an ordinary man with (what society views as) ordinary male desires, and in her struggle to convince others that her love is real and worth engaging with, despite society dismissing it as frivolous and false, too childlike to even be acknowledged. No, she's told by the men around her, even Erik, who should know better due to his own oppression.

You're doing it wrong; that's not how real love between normal adults should work. Do it my way instead, no matter how traumatic that is for you.

Now that I look like someone who's gone through testosterone-dominant puberty, I find myself often being read as transfeminine, because people rarely look at someone with a beard and a cracked voice in a dress and think, "that must be a trans *man*." I'm lucky that I live in a part of the United States where I can (usually) safely present this way, but it still causes a lot of confusion. Not only am I not supposed to be queer, because that's viewed as an *adult* topic, and therefore one that's off the table for oft-infantilized autistic people, I'm not even doing others the courtesy of clearly signaling which type of queer I am.

There's a particular kind of catch-22 that trans men face when deciding what their transition is going to consist of. Presenting fully as masculine can result in being branded a "traitor to your sex" or viewed as inherently aggressive and scary, but it can also be safer in some ways, depending on where you live. This safety is easily invaded by cis men whose misogynistic ideals don't discriminate based on whether you *identify* as a woman, of course, and the fear of having your secret discovered can be oppressive and destructive if you're going stealth. Our assigned sex becomes the madwoman in our attics, whether we want it to or not.

Sexual orientation is a minefield as well, as trans men are rarely allowed to just be the orientation that they are. If you're straight, people view you as a lesbian and claim that your wife is a secret lesbian for loving you. If you're bisexual or pansexual, the specific label you choose is picked apart and mined for gendered subtext by transphobic cis people. If you're gay, you're asked (as I have been) things like, "What does that even *mean*? Are you just attracted to other trans men?"

Usually, these questions come from cis gay men who don't want to let me exist in the same sphere as them, as though their lack of attraction to me was the defining factor in my sexual orientation. (I can't help wondering if they respond the same way to other cis men who just aren't their type due to any number of physical traits, like having acne or being short.)

If I've ever experienced male privilege, it was in such a fleeting instance that it never registered as any different or better than the various types of gendered oppression I've lived with my entire life. This doesn't matter to trans-exclusionary radical feminists, who insist I must have transitioned solely to escape oppression, but the experience of being viewed as a cis girl failing at gender, a "trans-trender" failing at it in a completely different way, and now a masculine person in feminine clothing has given me no such privilege. I never thought that it would when I decided to transition - it was a drive toward truth, not a drive toward privilege.

There's certainly another potential version of me, though, that found less tolerant trans friends and mentors on the internet and learned about transmedicalism in a positive light. If you're unfamiliar with transmedicalism, it's the belief that transgender identity is purely a medical condition defined by hating one's body and wishing to be as close to cisgender as possible. This is an easy belief to hold when you're young and struggling to make cis/het society accept you, but it quickly leads to lateral aggression and mistreatment of nonbinary and gender non-conforming trans people.

Had I learned this definition first and been presented with no alternate options, I could have easily decided I had to live as a handsome, fully unclockable straight man in masculine clothing, having had all *the surgeries* and rejected any and all aspects of queerness and gender non-conformity forever, to become a real man.

To fully embody the archetype of the ideal cis/het man, I would, of course, have to be misogynistic and bigoted against other trans people who didn't pass as well as me. If I were out as trans, I'd have to joke about Aidens and transtrenders and constantly reassure cis people that, no, really, it's *fine* if you think your sexual repulsion defines my identity; I don't care at all, it makes perfect sense, and you should never have to do any critical thinking about it.

I would have to sacrifice the heart of my own maleness if I wanted to become an ordinary man by the standards of mainstream cis/het society.

My family was so unaccepting of my identity that I had to run away. Even if they had been accepting, though, it would have been conditional. They were the type of cis person who couldn't spend five minutes around a trans person unless that trans person passed fully, flawlessly, always.

Passing, of course, doesn't just mean looking cis - at least, not if you ask a cis person. It means looking *hot*. It means looking like a conventionally beautiful cis person. Otherwise, flaws that would be easier to overlook in a cis person are seen as shameful failures. Why would I even bother transitioning if it meant I'd end up with terrible acne and a neckbeard? Why would I bother if not to shock cis men with how perfectly I meet the highest of all the high standards they hold for themselves?

Ugliness is terrifying when you're trans. It feels like a sign that you've failed to be yourself and thus failed to be a person entirely - because who fails at that, the most inherent property of being an individual?

I am not Erik, though. Erik is a character in a story. In a household full of other queer people who don't look the way cis/het society wants them to look, it doesn't matter if I'm ugly. Ugliness and beauty are equally accessible because I get to decide their definitions, and none of the people I live with will presume to tell me I'm wrong.

Some trans people are conventionally attractive for their gender, as are some cis people, but that's not the standard. Perhaps you've only ever seen three or four prominent trans people whose public image requires that they look palatable to a wide audience. They are trans, and their experience matters, but a glamorous photoshoot or a YouTube video with careful makeup and lighting isn't the whole world, and they are not every trans person in it.

In an accepting home, one we can turn to for sanctuary when the world outside rejects us, we can accept ourselves and take joy in our bodies and identities, regardless of whether they're normal. In a home that rejects us, though, we have to struggle to build a new home out of bits and pieces, decentered and unsure whether we can trust the people in our lives.

When we're not taught to accept and value ourselves as we are, we learn whatever lessons are available to us instead. Sometimes we get lucky, but sometimes things go horribly wrong, and we end up turning against ourselves and other trans people, feeling as if a transgender life isn't worth living unless it's indistinguishable from a cis one.

We should not be content with cellars, but neither should we force ourselves to be exactly like everybody else, hurting other vulnerable people who should be our friends and allies in the process. We can be people, we can be *someone*, but we do not have to be ordinary.

"Poor, unhappy Erik! Shall we pity him? Shall we curse him? He asked only to be 'some one,' like everybody else. But he was too ugly! And he had to hide his genius or use it to play tricks with, when, with an ordinary face, he would have been one of the most distinguished of mankind! He had a heart that could have held the entire empire of the world; and, in the end, he had to content himself with a cellar. Ah, yes, we must need pity the Opera ghost..."

— Gaston Leroux, The Phantom of the Opera

Author Bio

Finley Lockhart-Willow is a gay trans man, an aspiring writer, and a lifelong horror fan based in the Pacific Northwest. Horror was instrumental in xyr queer coming-of-age, and xe loves writing about the themes and characters that have helped xem grow.

From *The Omen* to *Saint Maud:* A Black Queer Revelation

Akilah White

For Mercy has a human heart
Pity, a human face:
And Love, the human form divine
Love Mercy Pity Peace

From 'The Divine Image' by William Blake

Amongst all the terrors that stalked, floated, or shrieked across the screen when I was a child, none could touch me in my everyday life, reach out of oblivion to clench my heart in its sudden grip like the image of an inverted Latin cross, black on a white surface. My first Catholic horror film, at least the one I remember as my first, was *The Omen* (1976), directed by Richard Donner, written by David Seltzer, with that Oscar-winning original score by Jerry Goldsmith. In a YouTube video on her channel Avey Reads, Olivia pointed out that horror was culturally specific—the codes do not always translate. Thanks to colonialism and the Trans-Atlantic Slave Trade, a black, preteen Jamaican girl in the 1990s knew enough about Christianity's codes for remembered scenes to make me shiver in my church's parking lot in bright sunlight.

That areshole Italian explorer Christopher Columbus claimed Jamaica for Spain, a Roman Catholic country, in 1494, bringing with him colonialism's deadly horrors. Smarting from defeat against the Spanish forces in

Hispanola's Santo Domingo, Cromwell's English forces invaded Jamaica in the 17th century, achieving victory in 1655. They marked it by destroying St. Jago de la Vega, the major Roman Catholic church on the island, razing it down to the foundations, and later built what remains the oldest Anglican cathedral outside of England in the former British colonies. A significant enough Roman Catholic presence remained that I attended a prep school, a private primary school, in Montego Bay still run by Franciscan nuns.

My family was Anglican, but Roman Catholicism was similar enough that I felt comfortable while being fascinated with the differences. Both of our Sunday church services were oriented around the Eucharist, the breaking of the bread and sharing of the wine in communion at the altar. Both of us believed in transubstantiation, that the priest at the altar, a conduit for God's power, transformed the bread and wine into Jesus Christ's flesh and blood through consecration. But my church's simpler, if striking, design could not compete with the larger, austere, high-ceiling cathedral connected to my school and its small yet notable sculptures that lined the walls. End-of-year school events like graduation and prize giving occurred in the evening, so my memories are tinged with a gloom the electric lights could not overwhelm.

In contrast to that atmosphere's severity, extended through the sisters' simple, somber-colored garbs was their revered Virgin Mary, dressed in white and blue. At our daily devotions in general assembly, children sang in a haunting minor key that our sins fit us for "death and painless misery, hell and all its torments," pleading to God for mercy. Reciting the "Hail Mary," the most popular of the Marian prayers, allowed us to end on a warmer, gracious note to a figure who did not seem to require the utter abnegation of self the harsher, masculine deity demanded. No doubt responding to her maternal symbolism, I was attracted to Mary and the special status the Roman Catholics afforded her, felt a special thrill when I made the sign of the cross as we asked her to "pray for us sinners, now and at the hour of our death" standing in our white and blue uniforms, holding our blue hymn books.

With such daily rituals at school, attending weekly services, living with an Anglican mother active in the church, raised to follow in her footsteps, in a country that considered itself to be a Christian state regardless of the constitutional separation between the state and religion, was it any wonder I believed?

I believed.

The scene fixed me to my seat as it played across the television screen. A freak storm's wind whipped the trees, the dust, and the soundtrack into a frenzy. Lightning chased Father Brennan, played by Patrick Troughton, and struck the trees in his wake to form a fire trail that forced him to clamber over a wall into a church's yard to seek safety. He shook and banged at the doors in vain as brass instruments brayed, choral voices yelped, and thunder broke through the cacophony. Again, lightning struck to forge a church's architectural adornment into a black stake. As I sat and watched it, flung from the heavens, pierce through his body, nailing him to the earth, how could I not have felt it, as if it had pierced my own? How could I not be terrified?

My rituals and beliefs did not seem a strong enough armor to protect me from such a dire fate. Perhaps I, too, would be with Father Brennan to "share out our sentence" in "hell, with all its torments." Why? Well, I liked girls as well as boys. By the time I was twelve, I had kissed both.

Without knowing the crime, the older church friends in my youth group viewed my mother's decision to transfer me to an all-girls boarding high school as a kind of sentence. They pantomimed lurid stories of what lesbians did in dormitories in the dark, employing whatever phallic object they could find to satisfy their abnormal, monstrous desires. I laughed with everyone else, even as an inner part of my growing self began to petrify.

I did not grow up in an overtly homophobic household or church. I cannot recall ever hearing my mother or aunt, who raised me, say anything bad about queer people. None of the Anglican priests preached fire and damnation upon us from the pulpit when I sat in the pews—that was more the Pentecostal's and other so-called evangelical churches' domain. Dancehall music, one of several new genres Jamaica created, has an international reputation for being violently homophobic, but I did not listen to it much. I knew Eminem's lyrics better than I did any local dancehall DJ's. Yet there was a general lack of permissiveness I understood and absorbed from birth. After all, I never saw anyone "out"; what I knew was the strange knowing silence around a much-beloved choir director. My aunt attended one of those Pentecostal churches. I knew the infamous dancehall songs even if I didn't play them for my own enjoyment. (They have long since been subversively reclaimed by parts of the local queer community who are the most enthusiastic dancers when DJs play them at parties.) And, of course, there was the socially accepted anti-queer horror or mockery publicly expressed in the every day.

Boarding school was where my queer self's petrification took hold for many years. Historically a Baptist school, it was government run by the time I attended, although there was still a church presence through the board of trustees. Evangelical teachers claimed the school and its students as their fiefdom, passionate and vocal in their faith, firm in their fervor to stamp out any sign of queerness wherever they might spy it.

I carry from my final year there another clear memory. One weekend day in the early evening, two girls were discovered in bed together in one of the senior dormitories—mine. Someone notified a few of the most zealous Christian teachers who lived on campus. They arrived, ordered us out of the dormitory, shut the green doors against us, and locked themselves in the room with the girls. The doors were not that dissimilar from the church doors Father Brennan banged on in futile despair as many of the buildings on the main campus dated to the 19th century when the school was founded. I remember looking off into the sunset sky, numb, as the teachers' shrieked their supernatural exhortations, committed to driving whatever demons they had summoned out of our friends.

In the many years between then and now, I softened back into my fuller self. I spent nearly a decade in Canada, where I thought I would find queer freedom, only to discover that it would not be as easy as I thought for a black, closeted woman to find freedom in Mennonite country. I had to truly want it for myself first. I might have needed to trust in the very white LGBTQIA+ student group that existed in a fairly multiracial university campus. (I did not.) There were complicated realities about Canada, not at all the harmonious multicultural haven it presented to the world, and about myself with which I had to reckon. I returned home to Jamaica in search of roots I realized I might have left behind when I sought to transplant myself elsewhere.

The lasting joy in my life has been the discovery that I could seed and blossom in a homegrown, largely activist, queer community, even as we all negotiated through the difficulties in being here, as queer folx do all over the world. A recent sign of the pleasure I now allowed myself was my response to *Saint Maud* (2019), written and directed by Rose Glass with cinematography by Ben Fordesman. A recent contribution to the Catholic horror subgenre, it proffered a revelatory space within which I could revel and play with its queerness, overt and sublimated, declared and denied. A Latin cross in any position could no longer pulse with power, and Maud's religious fanaticism fascinated rather than terrified.

O Rose thou art sick.
The invisible worm,
That flies in the night
In the howling storm:

Has found out thy bed
Of crimson joy:
And his dark secret love
Does thy life destroy.

'The Sick Rose' by William Blake

One's first understanding of queerness is through the body. It often takes years before one finds the verbal language for it through media and community. If lucky, it proves to be an affirmative experience. Too often, it teaches us to distrust established authority and societal institutions that define us as horrific disposable disruptions. We have had to be the authors of our own existence to survive. *Saint Maud's* title character was familiar with her pronounced lack of interest in external religious authority. Unlike more typical catholic horror fare like *The Omen,* in which priests, Biblical scripture, and God himself were pivotal guides, keys, or weapons to discern or deploy when needed, Maud's primary mode of perception, communication, and comprehension of the spiritual other was through her physical body. With only the aid of Biblical imagery as envisioned through the iconoclast William Blake, she refashioned a faith in her own image, within her own body, in isolation. But is there danger in such a path when one's corporeal existence is marked by severe trauma?

Set in an English coastal town, Maud, played by Morfyyd Clark, was a young nurse who joined a private nursing agency after her involvement in a mysterious bloody incident at St. Afra's hospital resulted in her departure. The agency placed her with Amanda, played by Jennifer Ehle, a once famous US-American dancer and choreographer now suffering through the late stage of lymphoma. Maud, newly converted to her own brand of solitary Roman Catholicism, interprets Amanda's polite curiosity as the cry of a soul in need of saving—the grand mission God promised her.

Rose Glass wrote and filmed Maud's story in a way that easily lent itself to a psychological reading. In a February 2021 interview with Candice Frederick for "Elle" magazine, Rose Glass shared that in the scene in which

Maud spoke to God at her apartment shrine, God's voice was Morfyyd Clark's turned down several notches. Further on, she noted:

"Yes, probably a lot of what happens in the film on a literal level is a result of psychosis and delusions. But the experience Maud's going through, even if that's just sort of the scientific explanation for it, doesn't give you much insight into what she's actually experiencing and why she's doing stuff."

Early on, I found that the most exciting path into the story was to accept the religious framing Maud imposed on her life and everyone in it. Then the film pushed me even further than Maud was prepared to go. During Maud and Amanda's first proper conversation, Maud haltingly shared, between audible, raspy breaths, how she experienced God's response to her prayer as his being "physically in her." She experienced his guidance as a "shiver" and a "pulsing." I thought of Amanda's earlier line, "No one sees what they don't want to," and had to see what Maud would not. She was horny for God and was eager to welcome Amanda into a holy throuple.

Once this truth was revealed to me, everything shone with transfigurative clarity. From the first conversation the audience witnessed between Maud and her then still silent but sexy Savior, her conversational manner suggested more a girlfriend trying to manage her frustrating boyfriend than a humble servant patient to heed her powerful deity's desires.

"Dear God, watch over me as I embark on this next posting. Think I'll have to get up at about six tomorrow. The pain in my stomach persists and is now further hampered by menstruation. I have taken two ibuprofen and milk of magnesia. Forgive me my impatience, but I hope

106

you will reveal your plan for me soon. I can't shake the feeling that you must have saved me for something greater than this. Not that I'm complaining or anything."

That first line was an order if I ever saw one. The mix of daily minutiae and passive-aggressive complaints about the glorious life promised but yet to manifest since their union was a pleasure to behold. This mix of surety and negotiation was quite common in older religious literature. Maud's casual tone, devoid of any reverence for a powerful otherworldly being, encouraged an interpretation grounded in a more earthly understanding of their bond.

Most memorable were the scenes in which Maud ascended to heights of religious ecstasy. Religious ecstasy is "a type of altered state of consciousness characterized by greatly reduced external awareness and expanded interior mental and spiritual awareness, frequently accompanied by visions and emotional (and sometimes physical) euphoria."[5] Rose Glass named them "godgasms" in an interview with Rachel Handler for The Vulture. All three scenes happened in Amanda's house after some kind of engagement with her. The first, and arguably the most abandoned, was after the conversation between them mentioned earlier. Maud left Amanda's room, certain she had just ushered Amanda onto a path straight into her open arms with the words "my little Savior" fresh from Amanda's lips. Moving in and out of the gloom through a blinking circle of ceiling light towards the stairs, I could almost sense her body trembling. Were her pupils dilated? Maud moved up the stairs as if even the still air was a stimulant against her skin. With heavy deep breaths, she

---

[5]Wikipedia, "Religious Ecstasy,"
https://en.wikipedia.org/wiki/Religious_ecstasy.

caressed the banister and the wall. Finally, she flung herself to the floor and arched in wild abandon.

Her second ecstatic ascent came after a montage of her rifling through Amanda's possessions, emptying all the alcohol bottles in slow motion. Maud sat at Amanda's vanity, tried on her jewelry, and sprayed herself with her ward's perfume as we hear another of her conversations with God: "Your presence graces the air, and I feel fuller of your love than ever before. More than enough to share."

In the kitchen afterward, a new round of pants began, the gasps getting louder as her hands inched around her neck, her mouth widened as if straining to accommodate God's physical presence, about to choke. This, more than any of the other scenes, moved me to think of her euphoria as a lead into la petite mort, a French expression used to describe an orgasm as "a little death."

The final ecstatic state was a shared one. Maud and Amanda sat side by side in front of the television, about to eat. Amanda's patronizing willingness to pray with Maud before they eat turned out to be the latter's spiritual G spot. The heavy breaths and catchy gasps start again. Like a true neglected partner seen only for what she can provide rather than what she desires, Amanda had to fake her way through this religious experience. She carefully kept her eye on Maud to keep visible pace and brushed her finger at the right moment needed to bring Maud to completion.

The converted Maud was not that different from the previous worldly edition. Midway through the film, Maud's return to her old haunts provided a glimpse into how she was before: a fixture in the local nightlife with a fairly active sex life. Such behavior would not disappear, especially with what appeared to be an extreme and sudden change. Mary Magdalene, her chosen saint, was another figure that joined the spiritual with the sexual. In Christianity, she was one of Jesus' women followers, one of his closest disciples, even in comparison to the main twelve apostles. [6]In non-canonical Gnostic texts associated with early Christian sects, it was written that one of the apostles was jealous of Mary Magdalene and Jesus' super close relationship. She was described as being the one he loved the most—he even kissed her on the mouth. This led to some speculation that they were married. Pope Gregory I, who must have been the jealous apostle reincarnated in the 6th century, misinterpreted some Bible verses, "conflated" Mary Magdalene with another unnamed woman, and declared Mary Magdalene to be a (repentant, former) prostitute. That was how the dueling narratives about Mary Magdalene as a virgin/whore entered and still linger in pop culture, despite later popes' efforts to rescue her reputation into sainthood.

[7]Even St Afra, of St Afra's Hospital, where Maud used to work, was a reputed sex worker herself. There are many different accounts of her life, but according to some, in the third century, she either ran a brothel or was a hierodule, a sacred sex worker in a temple. A bishop, fleeing from persecution, came along and converted Afra's' whole family to Christianity. Unfortunately, the authorities discovered them all. Refusing to recant her faith, in one version, the authorities condemned Afra to death by fire. She burned near the river as Maud burned near the ocean.

In the same Vulture interview, Glass cited the erotic in Maud's spiritual experience and in her past life but

---

[6] Wikipedia, "Mary Magdalene," https://en.wikipedia.org/wiki/Mary_Magdalene.

[7] Wikipedia, "St. Afras," https://en.wikipedia.org/wiki/Saint_Afra.

downplayed its relevancy to her and Amanda's relationship.

"The whole thing with Amanda being gay, I wanted to play with people's expectations. If you place a Christian character alongside a gay character, the audience says, 'Oh, it's going to be a story about repressed desires; her heart says no, but her body says yes' sort of thing. But I've seen that story quite a lot before. I thought it'd be more interesting if the roots of Maud trying to save Amanda were not at all based on her disapproval of her sexuality. It's much more ambiguous. There is an element of physical attraction, but for me, it's not about Maud repressing her sexuality. Sometimes women bonding with other women can take on this almost romantic [tinge]. I think part of her envies Amanda and wishes she could be a bit more like her."

I am sympathetic to her position. I, too, wish to avoid a perspective founded in a simple division between heart and body in a straightforward homophobia. All that I described before pointed to a Maud already embodying a more complex union through a third figure: William Blake.

Amanda gifted Maud a William Blake art book by Morton D. Paley. Blake was a famous 18th-century English poet and artist, a dissenting Protestant who imbued Christianity with his own personal mythology. I became acquainted with his work in high school through his collection *Songs of Innocence and of Experience* (1789 and 1794). Through his art and poems, Blake expressed strong ideas of what a true human experience of God looks like and how the British establishment—the monarchy and the church—corrupted it. Outside of the classroom, others may better know him as a nudist, "obsessed by sex," as declared in a September 2019 The Daily Mail headline.

[8]Blake's incorporation of sexuality into spirituality started with his parents. They were involved in a Moravian congregation with a leader, German nobleman Nicolaus von Zizendorf, committed to incorporating "sacramental sexuality" into Christianity. Under Kabbalah's influence, marital sex took on a sacred significance that required its own theology. [9]Pulling from a legacy dating to medieval times with The Book of Hours in which Jesus' wounds were drawn to look like vaginas, and the Eucharist with its concept of Jesus' life-giving blood, they treated the crucifixion wounds at his side as life-giving slits.

Zizendorf also encouraged followers to perform an "intense visualization of the physical body of Christ...to paint mental pictures of Christ's wounds, beginning with his circumcision and ending with his side wound, [after which] penitents fell into an ecstatic union with his body."

In another scene, Maud read aloud, from the art book, passages on Blake's more independently minded approach to Christianity, which he recommended over institutional denominations. Robert R. Wark noted in his book review for the Winter 1978-9 issue of the "Blake: An Illustrated Quarterly" that Paley included "illuminating paragraphs on Blake's relations with the Swedenborgians." Emmanuel Swedenborg was a Swedish engineer, philosopher,

---

[8] All the following information on William Blake, unless otherwise cited, is from Kon Rachel, "The Naked Truth about William Blake," ABC Radio, March 28, 2014, https://www.abc.net.au/radionational/programs/archived/spiritofthings/the-naked-truth-of-william-blake/5351684.

[9] Swan Emily, "Jesus's Vagina: A Medieval Meditation," Medium, November 8, 2019, https://medium.com/solus-jesus/jesuss-vagina-a-medieval-meditation-ef78367ac2af.

theologian, and mystic, known for interpreting Christian spirituality through sex, including his own sexual encounters. He believed that people had sex in heaven in the afterlife and that of [10]"the soul's highest, divine happiness as comparable to a sexual orgasm." William Blake read many of his works, although he later departed from Swedenborg, as he did with so many others, on certain spiritual matters.

For a long time after Blake's death, there was a reluctance, if not an outright refusal, to engage, much less embrace, the sexuality in his work. It started with his widow-appointed executor, who reportedly burnt much of that work that included drawings of vulvas as gothic chapels and figures worshiping an erect phallus. Yeats censored Blake's Vala, publishing it without much of the art he deemed too explicit for the public. [11]Still, there is much in what survived. Blake's open praise of lust and sexual intercourse is evident in some of his most prophetic works, like *The Marriage of Heaven and Hell,* in which he described "the lust of the goat as the bounty of God," or in *Visions of the Daughters of Albion* the "lovely copulation bliss on bliss."

My readings on St. Afra to Mary Magdalene to William Blake created a path embedded in the film which could have fueled Maud's creative energies to generate a more transformative spiritual sexuality than I had first

[10] Lachman Gary, "Swedenborg's Secret by Lars Bergquist," The Independent UK, October 30, 2005, https://www.independent.co.uk/arts-entertainment/books/reviews/swedenborg-s-secret-by-lars-bergquist-322953.html.

[11] Bentley Gerald Eades, "The Stranger from Paradise: A Biography of William Blake," (Yale University Press, 2003), 143.

imagined, with more ambiguity than Glass envisaged. But *Saint Maud* is horror, a body horror in which Maud's relationship with her own corporeal body, with others, was far more painful and destructive. She found pleasure in the intangible and pain in the all too tangible flesh.

It began mildly enough with kneeling on pebbles during prayer. Her actions escalated when the beautiful Carol, Amanda's lover, whirled into the house with a confident smirk and sauntered out with a fresh stack of bills. Not even Maud's temporarily successful attempt at ejecting Carol from the holy throuple prevented the escalation into self-harm. The physical reality of sex disturbed whatever serenity Maud had managed to claim. When Amanda confronted Maud during her birthday party, when she dared to tear the veil to reveal to Maud her true godly desires, primal and fleshy as well as earthy, Maud had to revolt. Her subsequent experiences, including rape, could only confirm that God's true desire for her was to rid herself of the physical body.

I traced my journey with Catholic horror from the small flames that burst behind Father Brennan as lightning chased him during that freak storm in *The Omen* to the full blaze that engulfed Saint Maud as she stood on the beach, lighter cocked in hand. I had conflicting responses to that final scene. Was Maud a repressed queer, violated, who felt pushed to destroy rather than accept herself? Maybe she could be a symbol, the more extreme version of all the violent zealots I had ever known.

Amidst my spiraling thoughts, I discerned one truth: I still held a trace of the little girl whose heart pained sweetly as she sang for mercy from an all-powerful god; a trace of the teen who once felt that one of the most ecstatic human experiences was to bear witness to a priest as they lifted the consecrated bread and wine at the Eucharist's climax as altar servers rang the bells and the choir chanted in supplication, "Lamb of God, grant us peace." One clear truth was this: When I sat in front of the screen watching Maud gaze at the sky, the flames licking her face, a small part of me burned in ecstasy too.

Author Bio

Akilah White is a Jamaican freelance literary and film critic, beta reader, and bookstagrammer living in the shark's mouth. Her writing can be found in The Book Slut, Rebel Women Lit Magazine, Inklette Magazine, The Quarterly Conversation, and the Jamaican Gleaner, amongst other venues. Her internet yard is on Instagram @ifthisisparadise.

The Ferris Wheel
Kay Hanifen

Sometimes I forget my fear of heights. I'll see an open-air Ferris wheel, get on thinking I'll have fun, but feel that discomfort and dread slowly pool in my stomach, and cling to the center pole as it goes up and up and up. *Oh, right,* I think, *I don't like being high up.* The thing is, though, if I'm in an enclosed area, heights don't bother me. I can fly or stare out the window of the top floor of a skyscraper without a problem. It's when a three-foot barrier is the one thing between me and a short stop after a long fall that my heart starts to race.

Being a mostly sex-repulsed asexual in this world is a lot like hopping onto a Ferris wheel. I always seem to forget my discomfort with sexuality until I'm directly confronted with it. I have no moral objections to sex as long as both (or all, if that's what you're into) parties give enthusiastic consent. I am just not into watching it on screen or reading about it. Sex scenes make me uncomfortable, but not so much that it ruins the experience as a whole. I just become a bit less invested while it happens.

Horror and sex, though, go hand in hand. From the vampiric Carmilla seducing the innocent Laura to the teens cut down by Jason Vorhees for giving in to their animal instincts, to the never-ending pursuit of the entity in *It Follows*, sex has been used to simultaneously titillate and horrify. It's typically treated as a vice which young people, particularly women, are punished for indulging. It's linked with violence in the way that phallic symbols like knives and machetes penetrate virginal flesh.

In recent years, it's occasionally been a source of empowerment. *Jennifer's Body* is the example that springs to mind because she wasn't a virgin from the start, and Needy survives the loss of her virginity. But in that one, the sexualized Jennifer must be taken down and punished for her sinful ways. Having sex is no longer a death sentence, and, depending on the story, can even be the main character's saving grace. In 2019's underrated queer horror classic, *Bit*, the power that comes with sexuality and vampirism is not the true evil of the story. In it, a trans lesbian teenager falls in with a crowd of feminist vampires. She meets them when a female vampire flirts with her at a bar, and if vampiric eating habits are linked with sex, then they have a one-night stand that leaves her changed forever. She later has actual sex in the movie with the same vampire, and all live to tell the tale. Neither are punished for their sexuality and deviating from the mainstream. The main theme of the film focuses on how people can use or abuse the power they hold over others. Spreading vampirism becomes a metaphor for sharing power with the powerless.

And then there's *Cam*, a doppelganger thriller about a sex worker who discovers that someone has taken over her livestreams and is posing as her. My sister and I were scrolling through Netflix one night when we came across it. Having heard good things about the movie, we decided to give it a watch. I knew what it was about but somehow forgot that watching a movie centered around a sex worker would mean that I would see her doing her job. And like that Ferris wheel going up and up and up, that feeling of discomfort grew as the film went on. I was actually more comfortable when the horror started properly than when I was watching her do her day-to-day job. That's not the movie's fault. Along with being genuinely enjoyable and well-written, it's respectful to its protagonist and does a great job of humanizing sex work. I just underestimated my own sex-repulsion.

As a romantic asexual, though, I enjoy a bit of romance with my horror, especially of the beauty and the beast variety, but I get taken out of it so easily by relationship dealbreakers. I have a distinct memory in middle school of debating with a friend who was better for Christine, the Phantom of the Opera or Raoul. Now, my answer is Meg, as long as we continue to ignore *Love Never Dies*. But back then, I was on Raoul's side. She thought Raoul was boring, while the Phantom was dark, mysterious, and sexy. Though I sympathized with the Phantom's loneliness, I pointed out that he's a grown man going pursuing a teenager after grooming her since childhood by posing as her father and that he killed several of her coworkers. But he's sexy, mysterious, sad, and a good singer, so I guess it's all okay then.

I also get unreasonably annoyed at Mina Harker's portrayal across Dracula movies, especially as they leaned into her having a romantic relationship with Dracula. There has not been a movie that has done her and her husband, Jonathan, justice. In the novel, she is badass, capable, and practically carries the team with her own intelligence. Though he makes the mistake of keeping her out of the loop, Jonathan Harker loves, respects, and supports his wife. For a couple in the Victorian era, they have a surprisingly healthy and respectful relationship while Dracula feeding off her is treated like rape. It's kind of icky to me that they lean into the forbidden romance angle with a rapist and his victim. If they must have a love triangle with a vampire as one of the legs, Lucy is right there. Mina is about as bisexual as you can get for a Victorian novel. I mean, in one scene, she doesn't notice her husband having a panic attack over seeing Dracula on the streets at first because she's too busy staring at a pretty girl on the street.

We've all been there, Mina.

One of my dream projects is to adapt Dracula in a way that does Mina and Jonathan justice while also being incredibly queer. In my senior year of college, I took a screenwriting class on book-to-film adaptations and had my chance. This was in the fall of 2020, and I opted to stay at home, so the class was mostly me talking with the professor about the project. The professor, who was incredibly nice and helpful, would often push me with the sexuality in the script.

Would there be sex scenes? Do you think you could make this dialogue exchange more seductive? This scene could use a little more innuendo.

It was one of those times when I realized how different I was. Having sex scenes in the screenplay hadn't even crossed my mind. I often forget that it's a thing that exists and people enjoy doing. Although I write characters in romantic relationships, I can only think of one time when the idea of a sex scene crossed my mind. In it, the two characters that had grown close to each other during their journey are spending their last night together before parting ways. In a callback to an earlier scene where one character tells the other that some things, such as kisses, must be freely given, the characters confess their feelings to each other and kiss. It could have gone further, but I didn't really want to take it there.

The best way I can describe my relationship with sexual attraction is that it's like being born color-blind. It doesn't make me deficient in any way, but I really only notice when someone points out that the stop sign is red and not green. When I pass an advertisement using sex to sell something or listen to a pop song, I don't notice the innuendo unless I'm paying attention. I don't think of myself as broken or missing a piece of myself because of my lack of sexual desire, but it makes things a lot weirder. Romance in movies, for example, can be baffling. People will have a single conversation and immediately declare their undying love for one another or will constantly insult and belittle each other because apparently bullying is foreplay to some people. Hate sex, cheating, and people being high-strung because they need to get laid makes little sense to me.

When you don't experience something considered a part of the universal human experience, though, it can be isolating. Sometimes, it can make you feel less than human, not because there's anything wrong with you, but because the world at large seems to think there is. Like anyone who cannot fit into our mainstream society, I find myself sympathizing with monsters in horror, especially the ones that only want to love and be loved. Because others see me as lacking in something when they aren't saying my identity doesn't exist, asexuality can be profoundly isolating. While the other girls in my class bonded over crushes in middle school, I would convince myself that I liked a certain boy just so I could fit in. The word asexual hadn't even entered my vocabulary and growing up in a slightly conservative household, I was scared that I was a lesbian. (Middle school me would be relieved to know that we're actually a homoromantic asexual, and even though our parents were a little on the conservative side, they've

119

mellowed over the years. Now, I'm out and proud with their unconditional love and support.)

I do understand, though, the loneliness of the monster. Because I'm aesthetically attracted to women, they tend to be at the top of my list of favorite monsters. I feel for the Rusalka, who kills in a search for justice she did not receive in life, for Medusa, who was punished for Poseidon's abuse, witches who are hated for their power, and the unconquerable Lilith, thrown out of Eden for demanding to be Adam's equal.

Lilith, especially, holds a special place in my heart. For someone so averse to sex, it's kind of funny how much I love this succubus and how often I use her in my writing. I've only ever seen one movie do her justice. *Pure*, Hulu's *Into the Dark* movie directed by Hannah MacPherson, portrayed her as a protective force who punishes the creepy dads that drag their daughters to a purity retreat where they must sign a contract to stay virgins until marriage. For anyone who grew up perceived as a female in a religious household, this film is cathartic in the way that it has frank and honest discussions about teenage sexuality and how purity culture is incredibly damaging. Lilith is an eerie force of nature, but she represents the freedom of choice in a way the men in the movie cannot control through religious dogma or punishments.

My first publication was also an attempt to explore my attraction to Lilith the succubus despite my asexuality. It was a short humor story told in the form of an advice column where an asexual woman describes the kind of relationship she has as the Queen of Hell's girlfriend. In it, I play around with the complex choices made in navigating a relationship with an allosexual as an ace. Because Lilith needs to feed, they have an open relationship, but the narrator is secure in their romance. In this case, a part of the attraction to the human for Lilith is the fact that her magic doesn't work on the narrator. People fall over themselves, drooling for the succubus, but they're just food to her, and the narrator provides companionship and emotional connection.

There's a theory that Jessica Rabbit from *Who Framed Roger Rabbit?* is asexual. No one believes that a gorgeous woman like her really loves Roger, and when asked why, she just says that he makes her laugh. She's sexy, but only because she's drawn that way and truly does care for her husband. When writing Lilith and her girlfriend, I drew from this relationship along with Gomez and Morticia Addams.

I adore a relationship where the couple is madly in love with each other. I tend to be less interested in writing the movie relationships where the couple bickers the whole time to show their sexual tension and then kiss at the end because they may constantly be at each other's throats, but really, they're in love. I usually give those relationships two months post-crisis before they break up. Instead, I prefer reading, writing, and watching the stories of people who love and support one another, facing up against true evil. I don't find these couples boring. When we're inundated with couples who seem to hate each other, seeing some sincerely love one another is refreshing.

Horror, though, is about transgression. It's loving the monster with your whole heart, even as it tears it, still beating, from your chest. It's a part of the appeal. Our society has a lot of taboos around sex and sexuality. Unless you fall into the white, able-bodied cis heteronormative category, you are an aberration. For better and worse, horror relishes in the margins. Though films warn of the evils of deviating from the mainstream, horror fans embrace it. For the span of a novel, film, or television show, they explore their darker sides, their stranger desires, the monster within.

Sometimes I wonder if my discomfort makes me a prude. Often, when women in horror are empowered to embrace their monstrous side, it comes in the form of owning their sexuality (which is a whole other witch's brew of issues). Thomasin in *The VVitch* joins the coven by stripping naked and flying. Julia from *Hellraiser* uses her sexuality to lure men to their dooms. And you can make a drinking game out of the number of times Bram Stoker describes the vampiric Lucy as voluptuous. It's an easy shorthand going back to the Madonna/whore dichotomy.

Except, I'm not exactly a Madonna, even if I'm virginal. I try to be a decent person, but I'm far from pure and beatific. Like everyone else, I have a darkness within me. The source of my personal darkness is anger. Anger at injustice, anger at the way the world is, anger because it feels like I can't do anything to truly help. Though I love many of them, I don't see myself in a lot of these villainous women because lazy writers tend to use sexuality as an easy shorthand for monstrousness.

Female monsters that use their sexuality to lure hapless men to their deaths can be great, but some variety would be nice. Bev Keene from *Midnight Mass*, for example, is one of the most loathsome characters I've ever encountered, partly because I've met people like her. Sexuality may make me uncomfortable, but I'm not scared of empowered women who own their sexuality. But people like Bev scare me because she's so self-righteous and condescends to people who do not live up to her high and mighty standards of what it means to be a good person. I'd like to see more villains like this because their evil more closely aligns with the evils of the world. In a country where the rights of queer people and people with uteruses are constantly under attack by those who consider us merely existing to be immoral, evil looks a lot more like the lady who promises to pray for you to get rid of the gay than any succubus.

In a genre where sex and violence are so often linked together, it feels a bit ridiculous that I'm slightly more comfortable watching a graphic death than a graphic consensual sex scene. One of these things is objectively worse than the other, and yet I have a more visceral reaction to a morally neutral act. But perhaps that's what attracts me so much to horror. It's meant to make you confront what makes you viscerally uncomfortable in a safe setting. So, I keep getting on the Ferris wheel, going up and up and up, and learn to live with that pit in my stomach.

Author Bio

Kay Hanifen was born on a Friday the 13th and once lived for three months in a haunted castle. So, obviously, she had to become a horror writer. Her articles have appeared in Ghouls Magazine, Screen Rant, The Borgen Project, and Leatherneck magazine, and her short stories have appeared in Strangely Funny VIII, Crunchy With Ketchup, Midnight From Beyond the Stars, Dark Shadows: The Gay Nineties, Wicked Newsletters, Fearful Fun, Death of a Bad Neighbor, Enchanted Entrapments, Diet Riot: A Fatterpunk Anthology, M is for Medical, Blood Moon, Terror in the Trenches, Slice of Paradise, Vinyl Cuts, and

Sherlock Holmes and Watson's Medical Mysteries. When she's not consuming pop culture with the voraciousness of a vampire at a 24-hour blood bank, you can usually find her with her two black cats or online at her website: kayhanifenauthor.wordpress.com.

Eat, F*ck, Kill, Whatever: *The Doom Generation*

Daniel R. Robichaud

Do you know what the genre needs to see more of?

Well, everything along the LGBTQA+ spectrum, for sure, but ranking up there for me is a sympathetic portrayal of bisexual men. Oh, we've been antagonists in horror and suspense fiction and the occasional film. One need not read too deeply into Richard Laymon's *Beast House* series to see the albino monsters there as the ultimate bisexual predators after all. However, portrayals of bisexual dudes who weren't trying to screw, kill, and eat (not necessarily in that order) the poor, unsuspecting hetero crowds seldom hit my radar back in the day.

Then again, I was coming of age in southeastern Michigan, not one of the coasts. If I had been, would I have seen something like this before *The Doom Generation* hit my radar?

I've been a horror fan for about as long as I can remember. Not just film, but fiction too. I have strong, loving familial connections to the genre. My mom introduced me to them, and I grew up watching scary movies on the Thriller Double Feature or reading cheap paperbacks with nasty, gnarly covers since I was in single digits back in the early 1980s.

And yet, throughout that lifelong interest, I did not encounter a sympathetic portrayal of someone engaging with their bisexuality until I was in the latter portion of my baccalaureate studies in college and already mired within the struggles around my own sexuality.

This was 1996 or so, well after the depth charge indie film I'm talking about had seen its short life in theatrical release and well into its subsequent appearance on video. Its VHS box cover featured an interesting image of a hawt Rose McGowan punching through the fourth wall flanked by two cute guys—one appealing to the shirtless bad boy image and the other presenting a quieter, shier seductiveness. It was billed as "The Heterosexual Movie From Gregg Araki," a writer/director I was unfamiliar with. That film was 1995's *The Doom Generation*, as anarchic and bizarro a flick as you were likely to find in the mid-'90s.

In *The Doom Generation*'s eighty-three minute run time, a couple of outcast kids, Amy Blue (Rose McGowan) and her fey boyo Jordan White (James Duval), encounter trippy, sexy, bad boy Xavier "X" Red (Jonathan Schaech), end up involved in a homicide, run for their lives, and roll on down some strange roads indeed. The three characters are on the cusp of that personal apocalypse, the coming of age that burns away the children they were and lets the adults they are turning into emerge from the ashes. This is at the heart of all three entries in Araki's thematically linked Teen Apocalypse Trilogy (*Totally F***ed Up*, *The Doom Generation*, and *Nowhere*). By the end, the three of them end up in bed together, Jordan hesitant at first and ultimately discovering a love he'd never expected he would. X is not just a heterosexual bad boy, it turns out; he's also into dudes.

Unfortunately, when our threesome is at the highest point of their character arc, some very bad characters intrude and wreck the place. A gang of Neo-Nazi pricks return after being effectively belittled, and they are out for blood. Their appearance is marked by a recitation of that childhood "so-and-so and so-and-so, sitting in a tree, K-I-S-S-I-N-G" but skewed into homophobic territory, and they have their way with all three members, beating one, sexually assaulting another (on an American flag, yet!), and ultimately performing their bloodiest efforts upon the sweetest, shiest member of the trio with a pair of gardening shears to the groin and a subsequent communion of vilest intent.

This was shocking. Still is. *The Doom Generation* ends up delving into Tennessee Williams' *Orpheus Descending* levels of savagery on a lad who had just found his way to sexual identity revelation. That two of the characters escape, and the third is left behind would resonate all the more strongly for me a couple of years later when young, gay Matthew Shepard was lured to the outskirts of Laramie, Wyoming, and subsequently beaten, tortured, and left for dead. I've seen my share of human and supernatural horror flicks, my share of sadistic terror and gory films, but Araki's film struck a chord that has yet to fall silent.

Some might argue *The Doom Generation* is not a horror film, per se. Even IMDB's tagging suggests it's a comedy and a crime flick. It is both of those things, and yet it is not beholden to the genre expectations for either. How bizzarro!

There's that word, again: *Bizarro*. Some of you reading this might be wondering just what does such a term mean in this context? Well, it's not a term that rose from film studies but from fiction. A sort of '00s spin on the splatterpunk of the 1980s, taking cinematic, musical, and fiction influences and throwing them into a blender. From this raw protein shake of genre and media influences comes the most wonkadoo stories this side of William S.

Burroughs. Writers like Carlton Mellick III and Cody Goodfellow made careers writing fiction that appeals to the genre, delving into the shocking, the taboo, the hilarious, and the provocative with abandon. On the film side, a movie like Quentin Dupieux's *Rubber* seems to fit the mold nicely. Are these horror stories? Well, yes. Maybe. Sort of. But such stories are also romances and science fiction (or speculative fiction if you prefer) and mystery and gritty-grotty crime tales.

They employ surrealism when needed or merely wanted. They behave outside of expectations, seemingly unconcerned about reader or viewer expectations. They are defiantly their own things. As a term, Bizarro entered the lexicon in the 1970s as a way to describe the strange and unusual. By the mid-aughts, well after this film's release, literary circles fascinated with surreal storytelling, decadent fiction, and the dark fantastique adopted it to describe the type of work emerging from outlets such as Eraserhead Press. These days it is synonymous with a storytelling subgenre that embraces experimentalism and weirdness (not to be confused with the weird fiction subgenre, which is focused on supernatural horror and "strange" dark fantasy stories).

Like the best bizarro works, *The Doom Generation* blends genre elements and does not shy away from healthy doses of shock and horror as it goes about its business. Yes, we have a trio on the lam, young and beautiful folks burdened with flaws and guilt, struggling to get clear of some oppressive force. That's the stuff of crime fiction. Further, it's a road story about a trio heading out of town and finding themselves encountering crazy folks and hijinks on a journey outside their comfort zone. This is also the stuff of crime, and its kissing cousin suspense.

However, the film also happily veers into regions a little too far afield for either of those genres. The splattery violence certainly hearkens to the horror genre, but there are three other elements where we see horror's DNA. There's a strange air to the thing, a nearly subconscious or subliminal yet wholly present supernatural thread running through the film, which manifests in several ways.

First, there's a plague of mistaken identity gags. Wherever the trio ends up, Amy gets mistaken for someone else's missing, former, or beloved significant other. She has one of those faces that seems to turn a bunch of switches in the straights who interact with her. One case of mistaken identity is a cute coincidence or contrivance. Several such cases mark a surreal intrusion into reality.

Likewise, there is a reoccurring numerology matter. The film is fascinated with the infamous "Number of the Beast." Prices turn up as variations on, you guessed it, $6.66. At least one address is that number, as well. This is non-coincidental, quirky, kind of funny, kind of eerie, kind of brazen. And another intrusion on reality. This straddles the line between the actual things experienced by the characters themselves as well as the metaphoric things we perceive in the film's language of images and dialogue. It bridges us into the next item: The descent.

Through the film, though our characters might be driving away from their problems, their course finds them heading down, down, down into deeper dread. The film starts in a club named Hell, and although the events following it are tied to the typical sorts of rises and falls associated with characters moving in the general direction their arcs tell them to, the film nevertheless charts a downward spiral from there to the epitome of loneliness and destruction. The beginning of this tale might be in a hell of sweating bodies gyrating to a *nine inch nails* tune, but the story winds up in a purgatory where two characters cannot speak to one another drive on. They are purposeless and yet recall the importance of the act of driving just the same as any shambling specimen of George A. Romero's living dead recalls the act of visiting a mall, tending a gas station, or wearing clothes. The film charts a speedy trajectory toward despair that is outside even the nihilism of most crime fiction; this is the stuff of spiritual horror. We don't need possessions, demons, or knife-kill cliches. When these elements do show up, they do so in unexpected variations. The mistaken identity thing can play like a reverse of the classic possession: instead of one character assuming the personality of another, we get one character being imbued with the physical qualities of another. The fellows who assault and brutalize our heroes are certainly fiends, if not outright demonic. As well, the film features plenty of violence involving shotguns, machetes, and those terrible garden shears without the need of a psychopath boogeyman.

The Doom Generation is as much a horror movie as it is anything else, and maybe more of a horror flick than any other genre. A shame it doesn't seem to get that label on the tin along with those others.

Maybe this is due to the crass dialogue or the occasional zingers that wouldn't be out of place in a Kevin Smith comedy of the time. Maybe it's due to the active artistic touches that hearken either to the French New Wave or colorful Italian surreal cinema. Maybe this is just a wonderful case of the viewer bringing their own impressions and experiences to a film. Admittedly, as steeped in horror and crime genre pictures as I am, the line between the two can sometimes blur.

I did not have the easiest time accepting myself. It didn't help that there were judgmental jackasses in the straight world I interacted with, as well as "helpful" naysayers in the gay-and-lesbian community I was a part of. "You're actually gay, but you don't want to admit it," was something I heard more than once. "You'll be happier when you just realize that being bi is kind of like being a tourist." Tacitly untrue, utterly unhelpful, and yet I heard it over and over. Do people still say these sorts of things? I hope not.

Finding sympathetic resources was crucial to staying sane. Thank goodness I managed to eventually find my tribe. Thank goodness for *Anything That Moves* magazine and movies like *The Doom Generation*, which came along when most needed.

Seeing a flick like *The Doom Generation* now, some readers might wonder how such a film with such a grisly outcome could possibly be described as "welcome." Well, that part of it wasn't, necessarily. The film's conclusion was not unrealistically grim. It was chilling and horrible and perhaps even traumatizing. It was poignant and provocative, and it moved me, roused a righteous anger while also chilling the blood.

Then again, this was the '90s, and I was already convinced I was screwed on the basis of my affection for and attraction to both men and women. If the wrong people found out I was one of *those people*, well, they would bring me emotional and physical abuse and possibly an untimely, unnatural death. That was just a daily expectation I carried around, which manifested in Matthew Shepard's murder. The details about Shepard's suffering still churn my stomach: He was left tied to that fence for hours, face all but unrecognizable because of the beatings and blood, skull fractured, brainstem cracked … He died six days after the assault, hospitalized but nevertheless doomed because the wrong people found out who he really was. The stuff of nightmares, yes, but also a cautionary tale to hold close. His case was the real-world reinforcement of all that dread about being branded The Other, which urged me to, *Hide if you don't want to suffer and die*.

However, *The Doom Generation* is more than its dark ending. Jordan's happiness and the script's quirky, cutesy touches along the way were so damned important. Yes, they set up the conclusion, amplifying its power. They reveal an important detail: The evil was in individuals; it was never in the journey itself. The narrative never painted Jordan's character arc in any derogatory way, and the process of his becoming turned out to be just the thing I needed to witness and process as part of my own strange journey.

Much more welcome than the ineffectual gay character getting splattered by a bus for shock value and/or laughs in Ronnie Yu's *Bride of Chucky*. Much better than the subtextual equation of bisexuality and homicidal insanity in a flick like *Scream*.

Now, there are two bis in Araki's film, and neither of them is the gothy woman so dominant on the video on the cover. She gets to share sex scenes with both of the beautiful men individually, and the men get to flirt and make each other uncomfortable while also grappling with attraction before they, too, get together in the climactic threesome. There are two bisexual men, each with a very different character.

I tend to focus on Jordan because he's freaking adorable. He seems like the sort who is true to those he engages with. I wanted a boyfriend like that. After catching him here, I obsessed over the actor James Duval for a while. In addition to turns in other Araki films, he makes a fun and funny showing in another delightfully bent horror flick, Lucky McKee's *May*, but he's never quite as perfect as he is here.

I didn't really want a lasting relationship with someone like X. From time to time, everyone feels the allure of those we know to be really bad for us. And everyone who's indulged such a lure knows what waits: on the one hand, there is a difficult-to-match passion, but on the other hand, there are oh so many problems.

X is kind of the perfect embodiment of the bisexual alpha personality that so many straights subconsciously fear. He does try to screw everything that moves. X is a selfish bastard, but he's a good fuck (just ask him), and he's charismatic as hell. Johnathan Schaech's turn as X is that of the bad boyfriend that seems just sexy enough for memorable bedroom Olympics fun times but turns out to be a little too broken to hang onto. Or to easily divest ourselves of.

The Doom Generation is the best sort of challenging cinema. It grapples with some big concerns while it entertains. It includes a pair of bisexual dudes, one somewhat more sympathetic than the other, but both interesting human beings. It puts its characters through the wringer, reveals a glimpse of authentic damnation, and leaves them all broken ghosts, endlessly wandering in search of the warmth, the vitality, and the camaraderie they shared and lost.

Gregg Araki's vision is cheerful and anguished, colorful and playful, and utterly infused with equal doses of hope and despair. *The Doom Generation* might not be a perfect film, but it was the exact experience I needed when

I needed it most. For those reasons, it's still sitting in my pantheon of crucial films and those worth sharing.

Author Bio

Daniel R. Robichaud is a bisexual author living and writing in Humble, Texas. His fiction has been collected in *Hauntings & Happenstances: Autumn Stories* as well as *Gathered Flowers, Stones, and Bones: Fabulist Tales,* both from Twice Told Tales Press. He writes weekly reviews of film and fiction at the Considering Stories (https://consideringstories.wordpress.com/) website. Keep up with him on Twitter (@DarkTowhead) or Facebook (https://www.facebook.com/daniel.r.robichaud).

Forbidden; Or How *Blood and Roses* Shaped My Queer Experience

Cristian Presgraves

Jersey City, 2020: After making dinner, my husband and I get ready to eat. While eating, we always watch a movie or TV show we both decide on (or that's what I want to believe under my pushy arguments). Since we've been on a horror movie strike, I convince him to watch a film from the 60s he's never seen. One that's important for me.

He accepts!

It's a somewhat obscure movie I discovered a while ago. It's not on any streaming service, and you can't buy it or rent it anywhere. It's a movie I can discuss with other people only because I've shown it to them. It's the one piece of media that has forced me to, more than once, follow the black flagships on the internet. This movie is called *Et mourir de Plaisir*, better known as *Blood and Roses*.

Released in 1960, it's a very loose adaptation of one of my favorite novellas, *Carmilla,* by Sheridan Le Fanu. I can't say it's perfect, but in my eyes, it carries an unmatched sense of beauty and melancholy. The release history is a mess, so a couple of versions exist, including a censored US dub. Sometimes, censorship evokes a sense of "forbiddance," like setting your eyes on something you're not supposed to see.

Showing it to my husband is anxiety-inducing because he's as much a cinephile as me. What if he hates it? Trashes it? I would be heartbroken! I tell him a little background as an introduction in case he's not into it.

Dubious, I press play, and we start watching.

Santiago de Chile, 1998: My relationship with horror started at an early age. I was around 6 when *Alien 3* was broadcast on national TV. My family was not the poorest, but we weren't rich either; all our basic needs were always satisfied. As per tradition, when a movie caught my parents' attention, they set up the VCR to record it. They paused it when commercials aired because you didn't want to waste precious tape on those. The movie aired past bedtime for my sister and me, but thanks to eavesdropping, we could hear some of their reactions.

Oh, wow, I thought. *That must be a very good movie. We need to watch it, too!*

Days later, the VHS tape had been labeled. My sister and I asked my parents if we could watch it. She was eight and outgoing, her maturity quite performative to convince my folks. My dad had no problem with it, but my mom said no. Oh, well. In your childhood, "forbidden" things abound. You roll with it since the main source of trust is our elders.

Still, I didn't want to give up. It was forbidden; thus, I had even more reasons to watch it.

One day, when our parents weren't home, we snuck into their bedroom and snatched the precious holy grail. If I remember correctly, my aunt (who lived in the house with us) was looking after us. But for some reason that slips my mind, we were able to watch at least the beginning, which was quite graphic. My parents came home earlier than expected and caught us right in the act. They weren't angry at all; my dad might've even been laughing. Yet, my mom decided that they would record over the tape. She wasn't scared of us growing up to be psychopaths; they knew that was nonsense. She was just worried we would have nightmares and be unable to sleep. If we had bad dreams, she would be the one that would have to join the insomniac kids.

Good call, mom.

Fast forward to 2001. *The Exorcist* was coming back to theatres. I'd heard a lot about the movie, especially since it became the adult's favorite topic of conversation. I remember the talk among the middle-aged people and their stories of seeing it after its release. It was something they never wanted to see again.

Oh, well, I thought. *I must see that!*

But I was nine years old. Forbidden yet again.

My mom was uninterested in the movie, but my cousin wanted to see it. He was older than me, so my aunt took him. When they returned, my aunt was shaking, and my cousin couldn't stop laughing. I was very disappointed that I couldn't see it because of my age. The thing was everywhere, on the TV ads, the news, and the papers. Just not for me.

About a year later, a whole new world opened for me.

My sister and I had separate rooms with our own TVs, and thanks to a more comfortable monetary situation for my family, we had cable! It was nothing premium, but we had so many channels to choose from. Isat and TCM became my favorites, and I felt like I was devouring so much content in such a short period of time. My parents were always quite liberal; thus, we never had a parental control code. They trusted us as much as we trusted them. Kind of a dangerous thing, but I'm so happy they raised us that way. My sister and I had movie nights depending on what was on, and a franchise we shared was *A Nightmare on Elm Street*. Still close to my heart until this day, we used to watch *Dream Warriors* every time we could. *Freddy's Revenge*'s gay coding whooshed over my head like a bird. It wasn't until much later that I realized what it was about.

When I was a pre-teen, I got into the alternative scene. My dad was a metalhead and started introducing me to a bunch of music. For a while, I dismissed the "classics," as I preferred 90s metal, particularly symphonic and gothic metal. Yes, I was that kid. I found it fascinating, but the question remained in my head: If that's metal, where's the *rock*? So, I started researching, and thanks to our archaic internet connection, I fell in love with 80s bands and the style the gothic scene carries. You see, there are some movements that were once popular in the northern hemisphere that later regained strength down south. Goth was a strong one, and I was becoming a part of it, inch by inch. I loved horror, so I felt like it was a natural progression of my weirdness.

There's a club in Santiago called *Blondie* that specializes in a broad variety of alternative subcultures. They had 80s nights, 90s, Goth, Industrial, Indie, and (actually!) Pop nights. Sometimes international underground bands perform there. It's everything an alt kid could dream of. Literally, they had something called *Blondie Kids* on Sundays: a daytime event in which they let in minors without selling alcohol. Just the music and the gathering. And I was there every month. My parents loved that I was going out to those parties, and they even dropped me off and picked me up from there. Can you say that your awesome parents picked you up from the club? Because I can. I was quite fortunate. I later found out the place was a very safe queer space.

I befriended a bunch of people like me going to *Blondie*; I keep in touch with a couple of them to this day. I slowly started realizing that maybe I didn't like girls, but I wasn't sure. I still fancied them, but I found guys way more attractive. Being in those alt groups built a bridge to exploring what was going on with me. It was a safe space with freedom of speech and open-mindedness.

As it goes with the scene, we were into vampires. It's almost unavoidable, as some bands were obsessed with vampirism, peppering their lyrics with references.

I read *Interview with the Vampire* before I watched the movie, and I loved it. It was very gay, but there was something about Lestat and Louis' relationship that rubbed me the wrong way. It was too unlovable, toxic, and almost predatory. Yes, I know that one of the main themes in vampire fiction is the predator, but it wasn't a step toward finding myself. I still love the franchise to this day, and the early books hold a special place in my heart.

Still, I wanted more.

I read *Dracula,* and once again, my brain didn't comprehend the gay coding. In my defense, it's not as clear as in *Freddy's Revenge*, or maybe I wasn't the brightest teen, so I was still unsatisfied. I didn't know if I could find queer vampires to my liking! I wasn't falling in love with any of these, or I wasn't doing enough research.

One day, bored in my room, I was listening to Cradle of Filth. Silly band, but so amusing. My dad was a huge fan, and even if I liked gothic rock way more, I still listened to metal with him. I started paying attention to the lyrics of both *Dusk and Her Embrace* and *Cruelty and the Beast*. The latter was my dad's favorite, and even if his English was decent, he seldom worried about the lyrics back then.

This British band is fixated on vampirism and horror literature. In *Cruelty*, I discovered that an actress called Ingrid Pitt did the voice for Elizabeth Bathory in a song. I looked her up and found out that she was in *The Vampire Lovers*, playing a lesbian vampire.

A lesbian vampire? Oh my, I had to keep researching! The character's name didn't ring a bell. It was unknown to me, but I noticed that the band had already composed a song based on her on *Dusk*. That's how I discovered *Carmilla*, and I'm so happy I did.

I read the novella in one sitting and was mesmerized. I was soon researching the movie adaptations. Though it predates *Dracula*, the novel had far fewer adaptations than the old Count. I watched the classic *Vampyr* and was quite disappointed by how little it related to the original story. I understand that having an openly lesbian character in 1932 would've been impossible, but I was still disappointed. I wasn't super into it then or now.

Next, I watched the aforementioned *The Vampire Lovers*. Is it weird that I was an Ingrid Pitt fan before I saw her acting? She was quite a magnetic actress, and it was a very decent adaptation of *Carmilla*. Finally! But there was something about the filmmaking that lacked the melancholy and overall feeling of the novella. It was like they knew they were making a movie aimed at straight people. The title character is way more predatory than it was in Le Fanu's work, and even now, it makes me somewhat uncomfortable to watch.

By then, in my teenage years, I knew what I liked, but I hadn't come out to my family, and I wouldn't for a long time. Watching all these things, I never felt like they were 'forbidden' per se. The reason is what I mentioned before: these movies were made with a straight audience in mind.

So, there was nothing to hide. Yet. A big chunk of straight men loves a lesbian film for gross reasons not worth mentioning. So, all my *Carmilla* research made me feel quite alienated from my introspective goal.

These doubts vanished once I found an obscure French adaptation by Roger Vadim. I read that it was a loose one, and I was afraid it would repeat the *Vampyr* experience. The movie was a pain to find, and I had to turn to…well… the black flag ships. The decision doesn't come too hard when it's an old movie that you can't find anywhere. What else do you do when you don't even have the option to pay for it? You click download. And I did; I downloaded *Blood and Roses*. Twice.

The thing is, the movie had at least two known cuts. One for the US and the original for France. Of course, I wanted to watch the original! Anything else would be nonsense. But I read in some already-forgotten forum that the American cut, even if censored, had an extended sequence that people should watch. And by people, they meant the ten followers of the film. Ah, good times.

When I had both versions on my computer, I watched them back-to-back. It was a life-changing experience. It was subtle; the music was beautiful. The cinematography was outstanding for the time, and it gave me feelings like the ones the author evoked. It was the perfect film to watch for a queer, confused teen.

It was a very loose adaptation, but at least Carmilla was there. And I still believe that Annette Vadim played the title character perfectly. The film has flaws, yes. The editing is not the best, and some performances are ungraceful. But oh, I was so in love.

The story follows the Karnstein family in a contemporary setting. Carmilla is not happy about the upcoming wedding of her friend Georgia and her cousin Leopoldo. After a firework explosion on the estate's cemetery, the tomb of an old Karnstein ancestor named Mircalla is unearthed, unleashing her spirit and seemingly possessing Carmilla, who starts acting odd and committing bloodlust crimes. The story unfolds like a love triangle, and, according to critics, the ending is open enough to doubt Carmilla's possession.

I wholeheartedly disagree with those comments, as the movie couldn't be more obvious as a metaphor for a failed coming-out experience. The whole thing is about finding your own queerness, being unable to express it to the world, and ultimately failing.

All the people surrounding the Karnsteins thought that Carmilla was in love with Leopoldo when she was actually infatuated with her friend Georgia. In the movie, the myth says that if a vampire loves another person and bites them, after the vampire's death, the person themselves turns into one. The last scene of the movie is set after Carmilla is impaled by accident, dying immediately, and it shows Georgia on a plane, the rose on her hand withering fast. How critics ignored all the visual clues and stated there's an opportunity for open interpretation is beyond me.

For this reason, the movie is more of a romantic horror than a full-on horror movie. And I like that. There's room for tender scenes, enhanced by a saddened baroque soundtrack and silent moments. It's a very intimate movie, and it was perfect for me.

In my room, I used to have printed-out frames from movies I loved, and *Blood and Roses* joined the wall. It was a screencap from the iconic scene in the greenhouse, in which Carmilla and Georgia share a kiss after the latter cuts herself with a thorn. It's a beautiful, unforgettable moment, and it's still one of my favorites. Their actual relationship doesn't go beyond that. There's no sex involved, and one could argue that, in general, it lacks sexual tension. Unlike other movies in the lesbian vampire genre, this is delicate and doesn't confuse the two. The sexual tension in *The Vampire Lovers* is exploitative, whereas the romantic tension in *Blood and Roses* is heartbreaking. Especially for how the whole thing ends.

As queer people, we understand unrequited love and how heartbreaking it is, especially if the object of our desire is not a part of our world. It's been cliché in fiction because there was a period of time in which we had to lurk in the shadows, like a vampire. High school was tremendously difficult for this reason (among others), so the movie was always there for me as a reflection of my own self.

I know that making a movie so subtle nowadays would be detrimental to the advance of our community, but in high school, I didn't have a sense of community like I do now. Of course, I'm freer and mostly fearless, but that doesn't happen everywhere to everyone, and that's a tragedy.

After watching both versions several times, I kind of turned into a *Blood and Roses* preacher. I tried to re-edit the French version with the extended US dream sequence, but since the latter was in 4:3, it was a whole mess. My computer froze so many times I had to give up. It could be an interesting project that no one has done yet, but I'm sad to say there's not an audience for it.

I stuck with the French version, and I showed it to all my friends in high school and to the goths I still talked to. Some of them liked it, but no one loved it as I did. They all agreed that the beautiful greenhouse scene was iconic, though. That was enough for me. It goes with the art subjectivity, and that's ok. It took me a while to understand that my experiences in life are the ones that shape how my brain interpreted the art in front of me, so my reaction to the movie will be forever unique to me. And that's terrific.

I used to watch the movie at least once a year. Now that I think about it, it has accompanied me through very different periods of my life. But one year, I suddenly stopped my ritual.

Santiago, 2016: After completing my Literature degree two years before, I got interested in theatre. I auditioned and was accepted into an Acting program in New York City. I still hadn't come out to my family, but since I was going away for a long period of time, I had to do it.

I came out with *Blood and Roses* in mind for a very simple reason. Up until that point, I had been Carmilla the whole time. Maybe people around me already knew, but I didn't want to go away (in Carmilla's case, dying) without them knowing my truth. I didn't want to be Carmilla anymore, and I didn't want to give false impressions. I wrote a letter detailing my experiences, especially in high school. I printed it out and gave it to my family and friends. It was a weight off my shoulders, and I couldn't have been happier for the reaction I got. I was loved and respected for whom I was, and they were delighted to see me living my life openly at last. Of course, it wasn't a real surprise to anyone; it seldom is. (I'm pretty sure that asking for Cher's 'Believe' on cassette when I was a kid gave it away to my mom). But my parents told me that they had created a safe space for me, and they were saddened I didn't tell them earlier. I assured them that it was completely a *me* thing, and I'm proud of them for the way they raised me. But no more secrets and no more Carmillas. I felt like my existence and my experiences were not forbidden anymore.

The day I got on the plane to JFK was my last time at Santiago's airport, and I haven't been there since. Life took an unexpected turn. I got married, and I'm living a great life. My family still visits all the time. And I assure you, it's much better when I see them here.

Jersey City, 2020: I hadn't been watching *Blood and Roses* once a year since I moved here. What an awful fan I am. Life got in the way, and even if I never forgot about the film, there are some rituals that vanish through time, unwantedly.

Since my husband and I are staying at home most of the time, we've been watching a lot of movies and TV shows. It was the perfect time to watch Roger Vadim's film, so I looked it up on my laptop, and it was nowhere to be found. I don't recall deleting it, but it was gone. I remembered that there was a German DVD version of the original French release from a couple of years ago. Now I could buy it; I could finally own one of the most important movies of my life. But it was discontinued. Oh, my luck. (Seriously, I'm still looking for that DVD.)

As it goes, I had to get on the ship again, but this time it hurt. I didn't want to do this again to my precious movie but lacking any other options, I had to.

I press play, and we start watching. It's on the shorter side and experiencing it now gave me a lot of memories I thought forgotten. In under 80 minutes, I encountered the same movie, the same feelings, and the same thoughts. But I'm a very different person now. I'm not Carmilla because my post-closet world is not her world. And that's ok. I still love it with indescribable passion, and I stand my ground, thinking that someone should restore it to greatness.

"What did you think?" I asked my husband.

"It's a *very* interesting film," he replied.

He's always very honest in his reviews. I had no reason to doubt the words coming out of his mouth, and knowing him, he actually appreciated it. Mission accomplished!

I still like the ending of the movie because it conjures up the literary works written in the Romantic era. To achieve the happiness that we deserve, it's the world that has to change, not us. Therefore, until then, we can't grasp that happiness. Carmilla dying without being her true self is tragic, but it's real. It still happens to this day. The message is not that she deserved her death but that everyone around her (thus, the world) must change their point of view. Her death is their fault.

Of course, this was the 60s, and we've come a long way. The amount of people claiming that we live a double life and our true selves come out at night has diminished abruptly. Most of us are able to live our truth 24/7, and we can finally see movies in which the queer characters don't die and end up living a happy life. Exciting times. But the battle is ongoing, and not all of us are lucky.

The main thing that worries me is that I had to leave my country in order to change the world around me. I still love my place of birth, and it's still my place. I love my family and friends, but I wouldn't be the same person I am today if I hadn't left. My life changed for the better.

Whenever I watch *Blood and Roses* in the future, I will remember that closeted little kid from Santiago, the one who felt his existence was forbidden. I won't let him go, as he's the reminder of the unlucky ones. He will always live inside me. I embrace him.

Author Bio

Cristian Presgraves is a Chilean-born speculative fiction writer. Horror has been his passion since he was a kid. He lives in New Jersey with his husband and two lazy cats.

Twitter: @CrisPresgraves

Instagram: @cristianpresgraves

Witness: The Transformative Power of *Martyrs*

Cat Voleur

All of my gay friends love werewolves. It was a trend I noticed back when I was still considered "the token straight friend" in those circles. Now that I've had my own journey of self-discovery and am openly pansexual, it's something I've started to really think about. Arguably, too much.

Don't get me wrong, I love a good werewolf movie from time to time. *An American Werewolf in London* and *Ginger Snaps* are both excellent films that I'm always happy to rewatch. It's just that I'm a slasher girl at heart, and creature features have never been my go-to.

When I started to truly analyze this seemingly silly factoid about the people in my shiny new queer existence, it made a lot of sense. There is a lot of meaning in a transformation story — especially if you're someone who has experienced a big change in your own life. Werewolves have this immense power waiting for them at the end of what is often depicted as a harrowing journey. This also tends to come after a period of denial and is accompanied by a healthy dose of introspection. This might sound familiar to you. It did to me. In a lot of ways, werewolves are the perfect allegory for people who identify as queer in some way or another.

But what if your taste in horror leans more to the extreme?

As a young fan of the genre who was coming up in the early 2000s, my tastes were formed in the era of torture porn. *Saw. Hostel. Wrong Turn. Final Destination.* For a time during my developmental stages, these movies were synonymous with horror for me. These were the new, exciting films that I had to beg my parents to let me see in theaters. Like much of my generation, my preferences in scary movies turned dark and upsetting very quickly.

So, you can imagine my relief when I eventually realized I was not being left out of the vital and ubiquitous LGBTQ+ themes that my friends get from werewolf movies on account of my personal depravity. In fact, transformation was an underlying theme in some of the movies I already considered among my favorite around the time I was coming to terms with my sexuality. *American Mary*, *The Perfection*, and *Raw* are all great examples of that.

However, that theme is never clearer, more prevalent, or more extreme than in the film I want to discuss here: Pascal Laugier's 2008 French masterpiece, *Martyrs*.

I have always had a deep fixation with this film that the people close to me just don't understand. Unlike the other titles to crack my top ten, this isn't one I can universally recommend due to its graphic content. I understand fully why it would be too much for some audiences. Even I don't watch it more than a couple times a year at the absolute most because I find it too emotionally draining. The content featured in this film is prohibitive to making it a must-see, except for in certain circles. It's dark, messy, and incredibly bleak.

Still, it was an important part of my journey. It was actually one of the last movies I saw while believing myself to be heterosexual. It wasn't a conscious part of my exploration, but the themes of transformation resonated so strongly with me. Looking back, I have a better understanding as to why that may be. I happened to stumble upon it first when I needed to ask myself some difficult questions about how I saw myself and how accurate that depiction was.

The extremism is what drew me in. It kept my attention. It made me cringe. I couldn't remember the last time a movie made me want to turn away while also ensuring I wouldn't. Most importantly, it made me think. A lot. My mind kept wandering back to *Martyrs* for years while I was going through some huge changes in my life.

The film follows Anna, who comes to clean up the crime scene of her friend Lucie, who has just murdered a family over breakfast. Lucie believes that they were responsible for the unspeakable abuse she endured when she was younger. As Anna tries to clean up the mess, Lucie begins to doubt that her story is believed. We see that her demons haven't gone away now that her revenge has been fulfilled.

It dances between the genres of psychological and supernatural horror during its slow opening, tricking you into believing it's one thing and then the other. It is only in the film's final act, after Lucie has committed suicide, that the movie reveals its true nature. Anna learns that her friend's story of abduction had been true. The family's matriarch had imprisoned Lucie years before, and the torture she'd inflicted was unimaginable.

The woman was part of a society that subjects women to prolonged periods of suffering with the intention of creating a true martyr. Since she already knew too much from being inside the house, Anna becomes the cult's next victim.

The pattern of abuse they put her through on screen is difficult to watch. She is chained, neglected, force-fed, and used as a punching bag in turn. We see the life slowly and gradually beaten out of her in one of the most upsetting montages I've ever witnessed. Only then is she deemed ready for the final stage.

This segment of the movie, the montage, lasts a little over eighteen minutes. It seems like an eternity when you're sitting through it. The brutality of the visuals holds little back from the viewer. I can assure you, it never gets easier to watch, either, if you are the kind of masochist to revisit the title.

It's a scene that will haunt you, as it did me. It's my least favorite part of the film, despite the impact that it's ultimately had on me. Because I was unable to quit thinking about it, I ultimately realized something about myself and my relationship to this genre that I love so much.

I am entirely unafraid of the pain associated with transformation. What scared me, what *scares* me, is my own weakness — the notion that I may not be able to survive change.

Perhaps this, too, plays a role in why werewolves never spoke to me as strongly. The full moon transformation on screen may be drawn out and gruesome, sure, but we know there's a wolf coming at the end of it. Watching *Martyrs* for the first time, I didn't know if Anna would make it out alive or what would be left of her.

This was a fear I had about coming out as well, especially to myself. I didn't know what my life would look like on the other side — what *I* would look like on the other side.

This is all very dramatic, so I want to do a quick check-in with readers. I'm fine. I'm great. I'm through the other side of the scary change, and it doesn't seem so scary or world-ending as it once did. It feels very natural, which I think is the point.

I was lucky enough to have people in my life who were supportive and ready to make me feel safe in my skin once I took the utterly terrifying step of accepting what that meant. I came out very casually online and was met with love and acceptance. It was only years later I was able to fully admit how horrifying the months leading up to that admission had truly been for me.

So, I'm dark and messy and incredibly bleak, but I am also fine.

At that point in time, though, before I had made the step, it seemed impossible. I suspected, rather strongly, that my increasing attraction to other genders was not going to be a passing phase. Still, I didn't know what sort of life waited for me on the other side if I told anyone. Probably not a life of living in the south with my boyfriend and his ultra-conservative, gun-toting family, which is very much the path I was on back then. My future, when I tried to envision it more honestly, seemed unknowable for the first time. That in itself felt like a violent change. I was so scared I wouldn't have anything recognizable in my life if I accepted a change of that magnitude. I knew it was something I had to do, but I didn't know if it was survivable.

Anna survives, in a fashion. While no one could live for long in the state they leave her in, she becomes the first true success story of the organization. Not only does she reach the point of martyrdom, but she's able to relate her experience of the process before death takes her. She does this in the form of a few whispered words to the cult's leader, Mademoiselle, and the audience cannot hear them.

When Mademoiselle is supposed to share this information, which they've gone to such great extremes to obtain, she chooses to kill herself instead. Her final words are, "keep doubting."

I do nothing if not doubt. Leave it to me to repurpose the last words of a fictional, deranged cult leader and apply it to my day to day. But it's true. I am anxious and am constantly overthinking my relationship to the media I consume and what it says about me as an individual. I'm constantly wondering why I like the messed-up things I like and why those things are so often different from what my friends and peers prefer.

Liking horror and being pansexual were, for a long time, such separate facets of my life.

I identified as a horror fan long before I knew I was a part of the LGBTQ+ community. In a lot of ways, I feel my relationship to the genre says more about me than my sexuality, even though they're both just pieces of an entire, whole, complex person. I don't mean to compartmentalize those two aspects of my life, but for a long time, I did. They were two separate things with two different communities where I felt I had entirely different standings.

In the one circle, I have always loved horror. Since my first scary story as a child, I've just wanted more of it, and it's a passion that's only grown as I've gotten older. It's something I can speak about at length and with certainty. My career has been built talking about and promoting this genre. It's the one place I feel truly confident. In those rare instances where someone tries to gatekeep me, I have the power to shut it down and hold my ground. I've seen it all, and I'm still standing

I'll admit that I'm not that fierce when it comes to being pan. Even after some years and a couple tentative op-ed pieces published on the subject, everything still feels like new ground in that regard. I'm shaky. I'm nervous. I often feel that I'm not really gay enough to speak for the community, or my corner of the community. It's hard to be confident about it because there's still some primitive part of my brain that feels I have to earn my place here. There's a lingering sense of 'otherness' that I still struggle to shake.

One thing I did after I came out was look over my preferences in media for signs. I had friends who, in their own journeys, looked back to gay characters they'd liked or same-sex characters they'd secretly had crushes on. There were tropes and patterns that would recur in their tastes and sort of foreshadow their big revelations. When I didn't immediately see anything like that in my own media diet, I felt like an imposter. As silly as this is, not liking werewolves felt like another sign I wasn't gay enough to be included.

Then something magical happened. *Martyrs* happened. Things began to click. I found themes of transformation in these extreme horror films that I've always loved. I found the insight and the courage to have differing opinions from my peers, not just as a horror fan — but as a queer horror fan. Slowly I'm learning to voice my pansexual horror opinions with the same confidence I would voice any other hot take that I knew I could back up. Lately, over the last year or so, there's been a blending of these two parts of my being that have made me feel like a more complete person.

It's something I love about the horror genre. There's a place for everyone. It doesn't matter how weird you are, how "other" you feel, or even how much blood you like to see on screen. Somewhere in the world, there's a creepy little subsection waiting to welcome you and make you feel at home.

I have done my best to line this essay up in a coherent fashion. I've tried to draw parallels between this brutal horror movie that means so much to me and what I was going through at the time I found it. In truth, very little of the process was coherent. It all happened in bits and pieces over a long period of time. Only recently have I truly begun to understand why *Martyrs* resonates with me in the way that it has.

While searching for a new label I could identify with, I didn't have the insights (or indeed the vocabulary) to express everything I was going through. I was just a person who was, in stages, accepting I was different than I had always believed myself to be. I was also a person who, like always, was obsessing over a new favorite movie. Even in all my pondering back then, I took *Martyrs* very much at face value. My theories about Mademoiselle and her final words all centered around the obvious religious implications of her message.

Does she want them to keep doubting because to doubt is to be free of a terrible truth? Is doubting the entire point? Are they approaching some horrendous justice for all the pain they've brought? Would the absence of punishment be somehow worse? This woman has been responsible for countless atrocities and finally knows the truth about what lies beyond. Is she trying to save her cohorts, or does she want to condemn them further?

These were the questions that lingered in my mind when I first watched the film. They're very good questions that make this extreme movie a piece of art by going unanswered. They also distracted me from a vague yet more personal implication.

Maybe we can't handle seeing things as they are without first accepting the transformation it takes to get there. Undoubtedly there is power in witnessing the truth — and that is how the film defines a martyr; a witness.

I believe this power, this transcendent foresight into the beyond, is extreme horror's way of concluding the transformation arc in lack of a full moon. The journey can be harrowing, but there is something indescribable waiting on the other side for the people who survive.

Author Bio

Cat Voleur is a writer of dark, speculative fiction and full time horror journalist. She lives in a house with a small army of rescue felines. When she's not creating or consuming horror content, you can find her pursuing her passion for fictional languages. For more information, you can check out her website, catvoleur.com, or visit her on Twitter @Cat_Voleur.

This Essay is Not about *Twilight*
Lee Hunter

In the summer of 2020, as the world was spiraling into the abyss and nothing seemed to matter, I decided to become a lesbian stereotype. I threw caution to the wind and reconnected with my ex, not for a steamy long-distance fling—that would come later—but for a virtual, two-person book club. It turned out to be a one-off event where we gave in to social media trends and reread a favorite from our youth. That old fave? Do I have to say it? Everyone knows where this is going. OK. It was *Twilight*.

I just want to make one thing clear. The point of this essay is not to bash *Twilight*. Even the OG *Twilight* hater, Robert Pattinson, thinks that schtick is overdone by now. Furthermore, I'm also not here to determine whether or not paranormal romance can be grouped in with horror. It's irrelevant here. I'm here to chew bubblegum and talk about gay vampires, and I'm all out of bubblegum.

Now that that's out of the way, I will say that I went into my reading with only vague memories of the book. I did have a *Twilight* phase, but I was not a Twihard. I knew Twihards. I broke bread with them. But I was not one of them. My best friends were big fans of *Harry Potter*; in fact, it seemed like everyone was…except for me. Not only was I not a fan, I hated the series with a burning passion, and because of this, I felt like an outsider among my friends. I know that's dramatic, but high school is dramatic, and so am I. I latched onto *Twilight* because it was something my friends liked that I didn't hate, a series we could discuss, and a string of movies I could go see with my sister that 1.) weren't Pixar movies, and 2.) were guaranteed to play at the movie theater by my house.

I don't feel the need to defend this short phase of my life, but I want to paint a picture of what I was walking into in the summer of 2020. I read the first book 12 years earlier and never returned to it, but I had seen the movies more recently (in fact, I watch *Twilight* and *New Moon* fairly frequently). I was seduced by the hordes of people who were reliving the *Twilight* Renaissance and relishing in how queer it was. I couldn't wait to discover any and all queer subtext and reclaim those years of my life.

See, my *Twilight* years were also my most closeted years, at least consciously. I knew I wasn't straight by the time I was 11 years old, but it was easy to put on the backburner then. There were no romantic or sexual prospects, and I didn't even have friends, so there was no pressure to discuss which boys were the cutest or the hottest. Don't get me wrong, I did have crushes on boys in some form, so when those days came, I didn't have to lie. Not exactly. But I still did. My crushes were always offbeat guys who were extremely sensitive or feminine. There was a sense inside of me that maybe I wanted to *be* these guys, but that seemed like a dangerous thought, so I didn't try to explain it. It's something I still don't fully understand or say out loud.

Instead, I fabricated a crush on Taylor Lautner. He and I are about a month apart in age, I was Team Jacob (at least for the first two books), and he wasn't the more popular choice. I don't think this had much to do with *Twilight* itself. It would be over-the-top to try to point to anything in the books and movies and blame it for the way I felt about my sexuality or gender. If it hadn't been Taylor

Lautner, it probably would've been Jensen Ackles or Jared Padalecki, who were also very popular with my friends.

Years later, with covid raging on and the future seemingly more unknown than ever before, it seemed possible that I could find myself in Stephenie Meyer's words and look at my past through rainbow-colored glasses. Were there sparks between Alice and Bella? Did Edward seem like a repressed bisexual? And what was the deal with Carlisle anyway? The closest I had come to discovering or celebrating anything queer in the series in its heyday was watching Robert Pattinson/Taylor Lautner ("Roblor") fanvids and convincing my friends to watch them too because they were "soooo funny." Every person on Twitter and their queer polycule seemed to be privy to something I wasn't. Not only was *Twilight* secretly and adamantly *not* cishet, but it had been that way this whole time, and these people knew about it since the ugly, homophobic mess that was the early aughts and 2010s. It wasn't fair, and I had to see it for myself.

I dove right in, flashlight in hand and ex by my side. Maybe I should've set my expectations lower because I was sorely disappointed. With all due respect to those people on Twitter (I'll never fault anyone for finding queerness in any form of media) they were extremely wrong. Not only are the vampires in *Twilight* the straightest vampires I have ever seen, but they are also the most boring. They don't stay out late even though they never sleep; they all have one partner and mate for life—after marriage—and they worship the nuclear family. Not to mention the whole idea of being in high school forever and the questionable implications of this...

I knew all this going in, of course. That's *Twilight* 101. I just thought I would find something that curved those straight edges, something that would make it worth all of the heteronormative, abstinence-only vibes of the books, but nothing ever happened. In fact, the book itself is a lot of nothing for several pages, not much action till the end, and even that is anticlimactic.

So, what did I take from this experience?

Well, it really made me think. Truly. It brought back a flood of memories of Myspace and early Facebook memes about how *gay* Edward was. Of course, sometimes this was gay in the early 2000s sense, the kind that would prompt Hilary Duff to appear before you and say, "When you say 'that's so gay,' do you realize what you say? Knock it off." Or the kind that simply meant young girls liked him. But sometimes, it was also in the sense that Edward was a sissy because he didn't kill people and because he sparkled.

The latter was extremely controversial. People acted as if Edward frequently applied roll-on body glitter before a night out, which he would never do because he never has a night out, and he is the most boring brand of heterosexual. A common phrase used by *Twilight* haters was "real vampires don't sparkle." Just thinking about that phrase brought back an image that at one time had been burned into my brain. It was a picture of the vampires from *The Lost Boys* looking menacing on their motorcycles with that oft-regurgitated motto across the top. It was an image that made me think *The Lost Boys* wasn't for me. It was loved by people who mocked me for no apparent reason, people who were really bothered that I was finding enjoyment in something that was basically harmless (or at least no more harmful than most other books and movies of the time).

In 2020 I was no longer attached to *Twilight*, especially after rereading it and finding it pretty unremarkable and boring, so I followed my curiosity and found that old meme. To my surprise, the vampires from *The Lost Boys* didn't look as menacing as I remembered. They looked beautiful and sexy and somewhat androgynous. They looked queer as hell. I knew I had to watch the movie immediately. I had seen it once as a young kid but had basically no memory of it, so it was a brand-new experience for me.

From the opening scene, I knew I was hooked. David, with his perfect cupid's bow quirked into a knowing smirk, has the kind of power I wish I possessed. He commands the room and looks like he might kill or fuck everyone in it, and either would be an honor for anyone. There is something vaguely Frank N Furter about him, just without the sneaky looks to the camera. Major queer vibes. Major "maybe I want to be him" vibes from a lesbian like me.

David's vampire gang is just as gorgeous as he is, and I found myself especially drawn to Marko. Not only does he wear a crop top and have a sweet, feminine face, but he also seems to take on a sub role in relation to David. Any order that David gives Marko—from picking up food for the group to pushing David around the hotel in a wheelchair for fun—he happily carries out with no question, grinning the whole time. I couldn't believe what I was seeing. This was the macho vampire movie that straight men and pick-me girls had been shoving down my throat for years?

While I had read *Twilight,* waiting for *anything* remotely queer to happen, I watched *The Lost Boys* trying to figure out what about the movie was straight. Of course, there is Star. What kind of feminist would I be if I didn't mention at least one of the two women in the movie? What kind of lesbian would I be if I ignored the breathtaking Jami Gertz and her absolutely magical, flowing curls? Yes, Star is very much there, and when she was onscreen, I definitely took notice, but her character just checks a box. Boy-girl love story? Check.

I'm not saying there isn't chemistry between Star and Michael (who is also beautiful, by the way) or even that Michael isn't attracted to Star. I just think that Michael is a lot like James Dean. He's pretty and handsome and brooding, and he doesn't want to live life with one arm tied behind his back. He wants Star, but he also wants David, even if he isn't aware of this.

David, however, is very aware. He spots Michael first and uses Star to get to him. In the vampire hotel, there's a poster of Jim Morrison prominently displayed. It's totally plausible that the vampires think Morrison is cool. They wouldn't be the only teenagers to idolize him. However, sometimes our idols are our biggest crushes, and I think David has a major crush. During his most intimate moment with Michael (when Michael is drinking David's blood), there's a perfect, music video-esque sequence where Michael's face is juxtaposed with Morrison's. If Morrison was just an idol, the power balance would be different; David would bow down to Michael. Instead, David is calling the shots, as usual, and his current order of business is getting Michael to become "one of us."

If we view the vampire gang as queer figures, it does beg the question, "what is the movie trying to say about queerness?" Are queer villains automatically a homophobic trope? Do the constant pleas of "join us" and "be one of us" hint at the "gay agenda?" In 1987, could the line "it's too late; my blood is in your veins" be written without the influence of the AIDS crisis? I don't have concrete answers to these questions, and I don't know if any exist. I can only speak for myself and say that I embrace queer villains. I can't vouch for every single one or pretend that there are no issues with them, nor do I think discussions about these topics are irrelevant. I just know that some people already see me—a real human being who minds my business, pays my taxes, and has never committed a violent crime—as a monster, so I might as well embrace it.

The Lost Boys vampires embrace it too. There is no shame, no apologies, and no prayers to God to save their souls. They are definitely not the heroes of the movie, but you don't hate them. Maybe it's partly bias because they're so damn good-looking and cool, or maybe it's because the only people you see them kill are a cop and some people called "Surf Nazis" in the credits, but you can't fault them for what they do. It's who they are.

There is someone who keeps you from rooting for the vampires, though: Michael's brother, Sam. Sam isn't a vampire, but he might be the most obviously gay character in the movie, from his "born to shop" t-shirt to his saucy Rob Lowe poster. And he's the hero. A young teen who takes bubble baths, sings showtunes, and is incredibly close to his mother, Sam is not the person audiences would expect to save the day, not in 1987, not even in the age of *Twilight*. My favorite thing about Sam is that he's very family oriented. I relate to him. As a kid, I was always trying to be perfect and clean up my older siblings' messes, perhaps because of my queerness. I knew that certain things about me would paint me as a disappointment someday, so until then, I had to be the best kid I could be, and I had to be a loyal asset to my family. It's this quality that turns Sam into the hero of *The Lost Boys*. He rescues his family (with some help), and he looks stylish while he does it.

In this movie, things aren't so black and white. There isn't one message about queerness or one moral of the story. Maybe the monsters are queer, but maybe the protagonists are too. The villain of the story is what really sets *The Lost Boys* apart for me. The vampire gang aren't the villains; their father figure, Max, is. Going back to *Twilight*, Max is the Carlisle of the whole operation. All he wants is a wife and a family. He masquerades as a bland "nice guy" in order to seduce Michael and Sam's mom Lucy, all so he can force her to raise his adopted vampire sons.

I've seen people say that Max is also gay because he's a bachelor who surrounds himself with beautiful young men, and I don't think that this is an unfair assessment. However, even if you see Max as a gay predator, his ultimate quest is to build a traditional (as traditional as vampires can be) family with the foundation of a heterosexual marriage. In this way, the cishet ideal is skewed and seems monstrous and ugly. In fact, when Max reveals this plan, he looks more grotesque and sticks out his tongue like a lecherous beast. It's the antithesis of how this family unit is presented in *Twilight,* where the bond between a man and a woman is seen as a vampire's only salvation. Instead, we want Lucy to resist this situation. One more point for *The Lost Boys*.

As I look back at this experience, I wonder if I've become the annoying men from 2008 Myspace comparing *Twilight* and *The Lost Boys* for no real reason other than I like one better. I hope not. I never expected to go on this journey when I picked up that book again in 2020, and I don't want to say anything that would insult 16-year-old me or the people who do find joy and queer affirmation in *Twilight*. If that's you, I applaud you, and you're welcome to tell me about it anytime. Maybe we can even watch the movie together because I unironically love it. A lot. However, to all those homophobic straight men who say vampires don't sparkle, you don't get to claim *The Lost Boys*. It's not for you, and I don't know how you ever thought it was. Open your eyes. Vampires do sparkle. It's in their blood.

Author Bio

Lee Hunter is a creative writing major who is finally putting her degree to use. She loves a good seance. You can find her other work in volume 4 of *Horror Scholar*. You can also find her on Instagram and Twitter @avoidancevoid.

The Intersection of Authenticity and Horror

Alexandria Leforce

From an early age, I was haunted by God. The first horror story is a God who demands sacrifice, but the real villain of the story is supposedly Satan. It's hard to separate God, Satan, and queer people in the United States' rhetorical and religious landscape. And the horror of identity, of the Other, is revealed in the Outcast.

My love of horror started off slow. It took me years to be interested in the genre, inching in its direction, and then falling into it as if horror itself is a different world. This world helped make sense of life, of feelings, of experiences. It started with *I am the Pretty Thing That Lives in the House,* where ghosts and death meet one another. Stories intertwine, and lives are lived simultaneously in different states of existence.

I was interested in the unseen, in the way the camera pans, how silence works. These are areas many queer people understand. We move our own gaze across the landscape in silence, careful in situations that can easily go wrong. There are spaces where we are perceived to be nonexistent—rural areas, mountainous areas, and areas colored red on political maps.

Horror started out as something quiet until I began to revisit my memories of Biblical literature and my indoctrination into religion from an early age. The restrictions started quickly enough, with certain questions shut down immediately. Whether or not the Bible itself is a thing of horror, it has certainly played an instrumental role in the horror landscape that greets people in the States. But the horror is often something quiet and behind doors, behind walls, unless it's at the pulpit or in the political chair.

We become strangers in our own houses, to our own families, navigating what safety might look like for us in one situation vs. another. The intersection of identities is often a set of societal definitions that make existence harder for queer people. I have become a thing defined by society—a woman, and that's where my identity ends.

The VVitch shows us that lived experience can be a dangerous sort of different that challenges the hierarchy. As someone who is gender fluid, nonbinary, I am often regulated to presuppositions of woman and how I feel about the performance of what it means to be woman. If I agree to the expected performance, even if I want to because I feel feminine one day, it seems to diminish the credibility of my claim of being nonbinary.

I exist in a liminal space where the term *nonbinary* still plays on the binary of genders. We are striving forward with our language and yet still tethered. I see that fastened experience in Anna Taylor-Joy's performance as Thomasin. She's utterly reliant on how society, in this case her family, perceives her. Her safety depends on fulfilling expectations, but she is seen as naturally dangerous as she becomes a woman, which eventually is synonymous with witch.

This fear labeling is something I am familiar with when hearing family talk about queerness. While it was taboo in my upbringing—I rarely remember discussions diverging to sexuality—since 2014, when the government decided not to intervene in personal decisions of what person another person could marry, it has exploded.

And so, the lessons of *The VVitch* taught me to talk to Black Philip when he shows up in life because if we are already damned by a God who's supposed to have created us as we are, then, of course, we are going to turn to places where we will be accepted. In literary theory, we already know that the Other often applies to queer people as with other groups of people that don't fit into the white patriarchal capitalist Christian society or fulfill those expectations. But this trope has continued to be timeless and how I relate to it changes as I continue to experience life in all of its facets. Horror teaches us to ask the questions we are afraid of; it teaches us to look at the shadow self, or the part of the self that society labels as shadow.

Often the first horror we experience is taking the first step into acceptance. My first steps were early in childhood until I, reprimanded, pushed it aside as a coping mechanism to continue surviving in a hostile landscape. Thomasin takes her first step when she finally asks Black Philip to talk to her. And why should we not live deliciously? What is it in the Puritan landscape that favors punishment and suffering? It's a mindset that still prevails in the greater U.S. society.

I was raised in the horror of believing that suffering created purification, that there was a purpose to the suffering. This suffering is often painted in horror films that push the characters to face themselves and/or change in general. The first step into the unknown requires a sacrifice of something. Horror films remind us that while horrific events might not have a meaning behind them or a reason, it is important to create those meanings.

The Other often has to accept their Otherness despite society's attempts to dissuade this. I have changed continually over my life to try to fit into molds and boxes

169

where I was never entirely welcome. The split from my true self caused direct damage, even if I did it to survive. There is a horror to denying the self its basic right to be expressed.

Claustrophobia is a theme in my life and *Mother!* presents it well. Living in a house representing an Edenic paradise, Mother begins her descent into horror as she's ignored, pushed into one metaphorical box after another. She protests the war; she refuses to hand over their newborn to Him so his fans can see it and ultimately cause its death, devouring it. Her screams aren't enough to get Him to agree to put an end to the chaos, and instead, he chooses to sacrifice his own child and her.

Mother is recreated at the end without memory to continue the cycle. She is molded into what Him wants. There is only so long for Mother to be put in a box before she ends up screaming and defying the expected hierarchy. Perhaps the most chilling thing is when Mother wakes up at the end, a new day started. I can't help but think, as a queer person navigating the world, that I did not have anyone immediate to look up to. There was a gaping absence, and I knew instinctively that I was not the first. Mother has no one to guide her; she must navigate this world on her own, come to her own conclusions, and step into her Otherness.

Each step into accepting Otherness begins in recognizing one's pain and suffering and understanding there is no higher meaning to suffering other than what we make it. This is the space where freedom is attained. Accepting that I was queer in a society that was often threatening to queer people is meeting myself in my own journey, looking back on what I've experienced, and understanding that I finally get to choose myself.

This choosing comes with its own consequences from families, peers, community, etc., many of whom react in fear and disgust. Or perhaps it's not met at all; this freedom is living our life, letting only those in who we can trust. We might suffer silently at barbed words, picking and choosing where it is safe to be authentic. There is no shame in being who we are and choosing where we express ourselves.

It always comes back to the Other and the need for Other spaces that, often in horror films, the antagonist (whether truly the antagonist or painted) provides. For a country that preaches freedom, freedom itself is often curtailed. The obsession with control of others is a thread that follows into the horror realm, whether it's being put in an Edenic box and saying it's paradise to the detriment of sanity or the need to control life's unpredictability and hardships by projecting all problems on a scapegoat.

The religious overtones in *The VVitch* and *Mother!* match the confines in which queer people must exist and navigate. If we do not step into the space of Otherness, into our own acceptance, we will end up like Mother who, in the end, burned and agreed to continue loving Him. Perhaps with queerness comes the need to snip the threads of love that don't allow the freedom of the self. Thomasin ends up killing her own mother and leaving a dead family to step into her power, with Black Philip acting as the conduit between her old and new self.

Queer people deserve to live deliciously, to have lives that cultivate prosperity, to have defined boundaries about how they choose to interact with an often-hostile society. To be queer is to exercise the deepest freedom, which is to be oneself without apology, to be under no one's control or influence except for one's own. To live in a world without fear of being who you are is a dream to most of us, but it's exactly what we deserve.

There's a type of purification that comes with stepping into ourselves. To do so, we must practice radical forgiveness for our past selves who may have lashed out against who we were in order to secure a place at the table, to have a roof over our heads, to claim family who might otherwise throw us out but are essential for our survival. We have hurt just as we have hurt. And perhaps we must enter Dante's *Inferno* "abandon all hope, ye who enter here." We cannot control the actions and reactions of others; having hope that we may be understood may be a dangerous sort of hope setting us up for failure. For some of us, we must walk through the inferno, risking relationships.

Horror is a journey of personal catharsis that lets us purge emotions of fear, shame, disgust, and even guilt. Horror is a ritual of the human existence that allows us to make sense of things in a largely chaotic world. We can put things in order through horror and process our own horrors that we might project onto the screen or the page. Many of us have already been rejected from pages of religious upbringing that alienate us from the support we really need and the acceptance. But stepping into our own power to do our own accepting is essential because we are all that we have in the end. We are not responsible for changing minds; we are responsible for ourselves.

Pan's Labyrinth is a maze of survival. Ofelia, the believed reincarnation of Princess Moanna, must complete tasks in order to return to her throne. Her lack of memory of her past self and not knowing who she is speaks to the queer experience. Many of us grew up in households that encouraged obedience over authenticity. Like many others,

I understood exactly who I was at a very young age, even if I didn't have the language to explain my experience. The more I found myself growing smaller and smaller, the less I knew myself until I seemingly forgot, until I became a husk of who I might have been had I grown up in an encouraging and accepting environment.

Like Ofelia, who is given three tasks to prove herself and to prove who she is, I experienced my coming into queerness in a similar way. Reclaiming who I am was a long road. There are some things that we awaken, like self-rejection, that do gross damage to our self-esteem and life. When I watch the Pale Man rip the heads off of the faeries after Ofelia makes a mistake by eating two grapes, I wonder if that's what I used to be like: someone who accidentally decided that for safety, I should eat the thing that causes self-destruction. It's difficult to look back and not feel remorse and regret, to think about opportunities to live my life at its fullest instead of being afraid.

All of these mistakes, though, have led me here. And they aren't so much mistakes as they were lessons to me. I now understand where in my life I cannot and will not compromise. I will not fill my mouth with apologies or make myself seem small; I will take up space. As I began taking steps to understand myself again, to let the lies to myself dissipate, I began understanding my experience better and began learning new vocabulary that better helped me explain my experience while unlocking a deeper perception.

A life lived without authenticity is hardly a life at all, and while we may have to survive a time where authenticity is not possible for our safety, the time will come when we must step into ourselves and understand who we are without any illusions. Ofelia returns to the throne surrounded by those she once knew and now knows again. This is what I felt when I stepped back into myself. I had known all along but lying to myself gave me the space to forget. Reclaiming my experiences, my perceptions, and living life as I wanted it by showing up authentically made life so much richer.

Horror shows us that through all the destruction, through all of the death, there are moments of victory in between. Horror lets us open up conversations into realms and ideas that are too often silenced. The release of shame and other negative experienced emotions can give us clarity on how we want the future and our present to look like. For me, being queer has been a hard-won battle with myself regardless of others who have entered and exited my life but coming to terms with myself and embracing who I am has given me a rich ability to actually see life as something full and worth living.

Author Bio

Alexandria is a writer and freelancer. She's forthcoming in *Air and Nothingness Press' O+EU*. After receiving her MA in English, she's been working on a short story collection. Originally from Knoxville, Tennessee, Alexandria now lives in Kentucky with her husband and dog. When she's not writing, reading, or hiking, she's expanding her oil lamp collection.

The Bride of Chucky: The Crux of Old and New Horror and Queerness Personified

Adrik Kemp

Coming of age in the 90s in Australia, as the internet took its first steps, the hedonism of the 80s bled into the alternative grunge of the new decade, and the Americanization of global culture began to be more pervasive than simply a McDonalds on every corner. The world started to shrink.

Now, we can go anywhere and see anything we like online. Even the COVID-19 pandemic didn't stop the global borders from blurring, pop-culturally at least. But in the 90s, those tastes of the unknown were more tantalizing, and we got them wherever we could find them.

As a child, realizing and holding onto the secret of homosexuality meant these tastes of lands far away and ideas so foreign to my upbringing were gleaned from the smallest of incidents. From foreign TV shows on community channels to music videos and late-night advertising for Adults Only phone numbers, all this media and entertainment reached its pinnacle in the darkened halls of the cinema. Only in the movies could we see such glimpses and representations of what it meant to be gay. The very history of film teaches us to read between the lines, decode the queerness from the work, and thus become aficionados – experts in finding gay subtext, even when none was deliberately placed.

There is no better place to seek out, discover, and be validated in such subtext as the horror genre. Now, of course, we are overrun with superheroes with hidden lives

175

and close friendships, and even open queerness, but back then, otherness stood proud and tall in the horror genre.

I would marvel at this otherness in the stories, too young to rent the VHS tapes from the local video store but not too young to stare at them. I was transfixed by the small, monstrous hand of *Basket Case*, starry-eyed before the ugly sexiness of the *Neon Maniacs* and terrified of the *Killer Klowns from Outer Space*. Nothing was off limits, and everything spoke to my inner queer. Systematic takedowns of everything being heterosexual represented, family, obedience, and tradition, all turned and twisted, so those things became the monsters and the outsiders – i.e., me – became the heroes.

Luckily, because books are not as heavily restricted as films, I found my way to pulp fiction bins and second-hand bookstores and began to read sexy, scary, but very straight and trashy horror. I graduated to Stephen King, Dean Koontz, and Clive Barker, and never stopped, so when I was finally old enough to watch some of the tamer horror films, my imagination had already exceeded what the silver screen could provide. Basically, I became even better at sneaking around, getting myself access to restricted films and seeing things far beyond my purview from an extremely young age.

This brought me to the most transcendent experience of my gay, horror-loving journey: *Bride of Chucky*.

But to first understand *Bride of Chucky*, you need to look at 1935's *Bride of Frankenstein*. This iconic film followed directly on from the original 1931 film *Frankenstein* and involved, alongside a journey of discovery for Frankenstein's monster himself, the creation of a mate, a 'bride' for the monster. The film was made and released as the Hays Code was introduced to Hollywood, which was a formal means of censorship disallowing and discouraging a long list of content from making it to the public eye. This included 'any inference of sex perversion,' which effectively nullified any queer representation for the duration of the Code and long after, relegating it to very muted representations of queer people and characters. To digress slightly, even without the Hays Code in effect, we can still see gay undertones (or some call them overtones) in other horror staples, including Freddy Krueger, particularly the second film in the *Nightmare on Elm St* series in 1985, which is now renowned for its gay subtext or the titular Babadook, from the 2014 film *The Babadook*, first interpreted as queer through Tumblr then gaining traction throughout the queer community on Twitter and through memes to finally solidify as a bona fide gay icon today.

Viewing *Bride of Frankenstein*, produced and released during the Hays Code, through this lens, unveils much more queerness below the surface of the rather heteronormative idea of creating a 'wife' for a male monster. Film historians also take into account the fact that the director, James Whale, was gay, as were some of the cast, so queer readings are almost certainly intended rather than hopeful. Take the fact that both the monster and his bride were born of the ideas and science of two men. That Dr. Frankenstein's mentor, Pretorius, was played with such an abundance of queer coding and subtext to almost pivot entirely into text.

The layers covering the queer undertones in this and so many other films are thin if you know where to look.

Obviously, from the titles, there was some inspiration drawn from this film when writer/director Don Mancini was bringing *Bride of Chucky* to life.

The titular Chucky was a character spawned from the toy mania of the 80s. He was the un-killable villain of the *Child's Play* trilogy, a serial killer's soul in a doll's body. Chucky's shtick was to manically murder children's families and then come after the child in one final battle to the death. And in classic 80s fashion, Chucky would return from the dead in the inevitable sequel, recreated thanks to the modern magic of manufacturing.

In 1998, in the midst of a grungy, alternative decade of style, this simply wasn't enough. So, creator Don Mancini, envisaged a film that paid homage not only to the previous films in the series but to the concept of horror and high camp in what is often called the greatest sequel ever made, *Bride of Frankenstein*.

In the 90s, many horror film franchises were taking the next leap and placing their killers in unfamiliar circumstances, namely, sending them to space. Notably, *Hellraiser*, *Leprechaun,* and *Friday the 13th* all sent their villains into space with little reasoning and high camp value, but other than the setting, they remained formulaic.

Unlike these examples, *Bride of Chucky* chose a different path and brought in a second lead to a series that had ended seven years earlier and was seemingly dead in the water, reigniting interest in the franchise for a new audience.

Having now seen the film countless times and having gained the unfortunate for others and joyous for myself ability to lip-synch almost the entire film's dialogue and soundtrack, I can assure you that every frame of this film is worth dissecting at one point or another.

They began by casting Jennifer Tilly as the Bride, herself, Tiffany Valentine. Tilly was already a lesbian icon, having starred alongside Gina Gershon in 1996's *Bound*, directed by The Wachowskis. The casting could not have been more perfect, with Tilly portraying a more amped-up, sexually ambiguous, blonde version of Violet from *Bound*.

Tiffany is an outsider. She lives in a trailer park in a mobile home with a gothic aesthetic, complete with a claw-footed bathtub and a pet tarantula. She is single-minded in her desire to be reunited with the love of her life, a serial killer who just happened to have his soul transferred into a certain doll.

One of the moments in the film I identified with most occurs when Tiffany's casual lover, Damian (played by trans actor Alexis Arquette), appeared following her seeming failure to resurrect Chucky. She ties him up and starts to play with him when she realises that Chucky's body is gone. The game of seductive and murderous cat and mouse that ensues, followed by an argument of epic proportions and Tiffany crying herself to sleep, were not the things that stayed with me, however. It was the image of Arquette slipping off his clothing and presenting himself, subjugated and seductive before Tilly, who held all the power. The following day, when she almost sexually assaults her stereotypically sexy, young, shirtless neighbor, Jesse, getting him to help her move a body in a chest also stood out for me. On the whole, the portrayal of sexualized men in *Bride of Chucky* was something of an epiphany.

Of course, this examination of the body only becomes more overt as the film progresses, and both Chucky and Tiffany express their desires to take over the bodies of this neighbor and his girlfriend.

But first, we need to rewind to Tiffany's resurrection of Chucky. Here, she becomes Frankenstein, creating her monster, and shortly after, when she is murdered by her creation, she also becomes the Bride of Frankenstein as Chucky transfers her dying soul into that of a bridal doll she has purchased Chucky as a gag gift.

Tilly's reintroduction as the voice of the new doll, a female counterpart to Chucky, is the highest camp sequence of the film. She is mortified and enraged – rightly so after being murdered – but mainly due to her appearance. Gone are her bleach blonde locks, her makeup, the tattoo on her breast, and her fashion. And so the first thing she needs to do is reinvent herself once again through the art of the makeover montage set to *Call Me* by Blondie. After close-ups of her hair, her nails, her tattoo, and necklace, we get a full pan from boots to the top of her head as she lights a cigarette and utters the line, "Barbie, eat your heart out," as Chucky's monstrous, stitched-together face watches on, enraptured.

It's the transformation from dowdy doll to gothic, alternative bombshell that in the queer community, we see so often portrayed by drag queens, who play with the idea of hetero conformity and perceived normalcy in so many ways and whose art form proudly celebrates the beauty of otherness. Although I was a few years from understanding this for myself, the seed of this idea was planted in my chest to be remembered and adored at a later, more enlightened time.

There are two more pivotal moments to unpack. The first of which is in a mobile home that has been co-opted from a roaming older couple (now dead in a cupboard), containing Chucky, Tiffany, and their two hostages: the neighbor, Jesse and his girlfriend Jade, whom they plan to switch bodies with once they obtain an amulet buried with Chucky's original corpse.

Tiffany has gone into full housewife mode, cooking food to serve up for Chucky while he holds a gun to Jesse, who drives them to their destination. Jade is in Tiffany's ear, whispering about how Chucky doesn't deserve her, and Jesse is in Chucky's, pointing out the mess she's making. As he criticizes her process, she blows her top and exclaims, "Here I am, slaving over a hot stove, making cookies, making Swedish meatballs, and for what? For a man who doesn't appreciate me. For a man who can't even wash one fucking dish. For a man who isn't even a man at all where it counts, if you catch my drift," and then she directs this part to Jade, "Take it from me, honey, plastic is no substitute for a nice hunk of wood."

And with that, the mic is dropped, and the two become enemies once again. It is her outburst against the misogyny of Chucky's behavior and the ideals of 'man and wife,' that she somehow wants to fit into but cannot, that again held hidden subtext for me. At the time, I was still very much in the closet and had been for years. I stared out, hoping no one knew my secret, wanting so badly to be part of society but unable to figure out how to do it. I was Tiffany at this moment, fighting the patriarchy and being knocked down by it as she is overpowered and burned alive (in doll version) in the very oven she has been slaving over.

But as with Chucky, she isn't out for the count yet, and, thanks to Jade, is brought to the cemetery to finish the job once and for all. As she holds onto Chucky's leg in a position of recline that is reminiscent of Fay Wray in the original *King Kong* and is brought into an embrace, she stabs him in the back before being flung away and uttering a line lifted straight from *Bride of Frankenstein*, "Don't you see? We belong dead."

This film taught me that horror didn't have to be serious all the time. It could be camp and fun and feature characters out of the ordinary. It was an experience far freer and more exciting than that of most mainstream media. It played with the genre and with the rules of society. It could take something that had come before and twist it to suit a new audience and a new time. Wasn't that exactly what I was doing with my very existence? To be so different, and at the time, still quite maligned by most of society, and to want to break it and reform it in a shape to which I was comfortable? This was what *Bride of Chucky* and horror, on the whole, meant to me. Everything I ever wanted was there on the screen, waiting for me to come and take it.

Tiffany Valentine and the *Bride of Chucky* film wasn't a finite moment of realization of this. However, in hindsight, everything presented within the film appears to be designed by and for a queer eye. It's little wonder it had such a profound impact on my teenaged self and continues to resonate through the decades today.

Author Bio

Adrik Kemp is an award-winning writer and author of horror, speculative fiction, and fantasy short stories and novels. He has short stories out in a number of publications, including Aurealis Magazine, Third Flatiron, Transmundane Press, CSFG Press, Alban Lake Publishing, and Pride Publishing.

Oh, the Horror!

Luis Johanna Nieves

My mother violently cried when I came out to her. Hot tears of frustration, anger, and sorrow painted her face. I wondered why she was so upset at me, her only boy.

Would she be like the mothers I read about? Would she follow in the footsteps of Victor Frankenstein and abandon her sole creation, tossing me to the wild where I would not survive? No, my mom was better than that. She truly loved the Adam of her labors and would not let Nature reclaim me.

I sat up in my bed, watching the streams continue to pour down her face as she professed her deep adoration for me. The emotions did not seem to match. I was left confused.

She grabbed me as if someone would snatch me from her. Her grip tightened as her wailing filled the room. I wondered how much noise my four walls could contain before they gave up.

Looking around the room as if I was in immediate danger, she managed to choke out a few words through her heaves, "I don't want anyone to hurt my baby."

As is the case with many like myself, I am and was always close to my mother. After some time of processing her feelings, she related to me that she knew for some time I was gay. Ma, as I affectionally refer to her, was simply waiting for me to be honest, not just with myself, but with the woman who crafted me.

The biggest fear in coming out was the impact it would have on our relationship. Being an only child, I was my parents' center of attention from the start. My father, who I have called Papote from an early age, knew I was a sensitive thing with a big heart and treated me accordingly. It's not that one parent was better than the other; it might just have been the natural push that led me to become a Mama's Boy, a title I have always worn with pride.

Is there anything more stomach-turning than a boy who rejects his mother or a mother who leaves her son to be feasted upon by wolves? Are our mothers not our first true love? Is a mother not destined, as Norman Bates told Marion Crane, to be her boy's best friend? Who would be so cruel to break that beautiful and expected bond?

The only downside to my revelation was Ma's anxiety over my safety. Our community was and still is twenty or so years beyond the general consensus of social issues and such. A freshman in high school was not immune to the cruelty and judgment of old white women who thought themselves and their cheating, bored husbands holier than thou. These were things I failed to be aware of or even knew existed.

While she was with me, she could shield me from such ugliness. What was she to do when I was alone? The children of those hideous couples had sharper teeth than their creators. Was there a place outside of our home where I could feel and be safe?

*   *   *

There was a flea market we would visit every Sunday morning when I was a young child. We weren't the church-going type—Papote never trusted them due to an overabundance of human error. That didn't mean my family wasn't spiritual. If you shook me and inquired of my religious beliefs, I would most likely just label myself a Catholic, as the majority of Puerto Ricans would do in that given situation or everyday life. Sunday mornings were not reserved for church, so we were blessed to be able to spend them at our leisure.

The flea market had an indoor section that housed small specialty shops. There was one that sold new and used video games, another featured candy and freshly roasted peanuts. Yet another had worn-out leather jackets with deep creases and cuts, and of course, there was a used book shop that doubled as a magazine rack. That was all fine and dandy, but my favorite section of the market lay outside the comforts of the air-conditioned hallways—the outside tables where vendors would peddle their random assortments of toys, antiques, and such. It was a wasteland of treasure that I explored during my childhood and well into my teenage years alongside my fellow voyagers, Ma and Papote.

Ever since I knew what I was looking at, I was attracted to the gorgeously vile artwork of horror VHS cassettes. These things littered the majority of the tables we would stroll past. Some would catch my attention, and others would repulse me to the point of aversion.

I tended to be easily frightened, but I pushed myself in hopes of building tolerance and appreciation of the scary. Sometimes it would work, but other times it proved to be near fatal!

Ma was a closeted horror hound. I only label her as such because she wasn't very open about the hobby, as Papote loathed all things tense, grotesque, or any combination of the two.

One day, while I was in the living room building my latest Lego set with Papote, I remembered I left a crucial piece—the instructions—-in my parents' room. Before Papote could stop me, I dashed into the room and was struck frozen at what was on the TV. It was a cackling, rotting face with the clearest blue eyes I'd ever seen. He—it?—lacked a nose. I forced my lids to stay open, gasping at the sight until I could bear it no longer. My body shut out the visuals as Ma kindly shooed me away back to the safety of the living room and my Legos. I had just survived an encounter with the one and only Cryptkeeper!

To paraphrase the great Dr. Frank-n-Furter, I tasted blood and wanted more. After a conversation with my parents, they agreed to ease me into the genre, step-by-step. My gateway drug? R.L. Stine's *Goosebumps* series. My parents used the situation to their advantage: I would receive one novel from the series every Friday from Barnes and Noble, with the expectation that I would read it before the next trip the following week. It would be a cycle of spookiness and reading. Our agreement worked, and the tolerance grew and grew. Eventually, tales of twelve-year-olds battling evil sponges under their sink or being turned into chickens by prankster witches were not enough. I was famished for the next step.

Although you're not supposed to judge a book by its cover, I would judge the VHS cassettes by theirs. And harshly at that! In my search for the next great fright, I chose to scour the flea market every Sunday for whatever offerings they had.

I found a copy of *The Exorcist*; its dull purple letters caught my attention, but the tagline proclaiming it to be the scariest movie ever made was what intrigued me most. Ma promptly turned that down, saying it would be a journey I would have to wait to take until later in life. I had no choice but to oblige. *The Exorcist* would have to wait for me, and in that time, it would grow in legend. Countless other films were dismissed for being too much for my tender mind and heart. From *The Shining* to *The Burning*, it seemed I would have to revert back to the childish frights resting in my backpack.

During one of our Sunday morning meanders, I stumbled upon a cover that held my gaze. A young girl—couldn't have been more than 6 or 7—kneeled down in front of a television set, pressing her hands onto the screen that was filled with nothing but fuzz. A cascade of hair obscured her figure. Staring at the image, I could hear the static. I could feel the tickling cling of the television set, as I imagined the young girl would. An interesting image it was, but the more I digested it, the more I assumed it couldn't be scary. Where were the sharp fangs? Where was the color? And the title? *Poltergeist*? I had no clue what that meant! I couldn't even pronounce it. My eyes strayed.

Yet another week passed, and the market once more beckoned us. With my latest *Goosebump* book in tow, I did my best to keep up with my parents, but walking and reading is a feat that's far from easy, especially when burdened by preteen clumsiness. With no foreseeable or attainable next step in horror, I felt it was only fitting that I head back to my origins and continue on with Stine's stories. Occasionally I would peek over *The Beast from the East* to offer a "sorry" to anyone I bumped into or to see where my parents were headed next. And for the most part, it worked.

It was during one of these glances that I happened upon another VHS cover that drew my interest. It was similar to *Poltergeist*, but it featured color! Though the case was aged and torn, I was able to make out the image of a girl, slightly older than the previous, looking up at an ominous high-rise in the city. The same waterfall of hair was behind her. Assuming it was a rip-off of a film I dismissed, I was about to bury my nose back into my book when I noticed the Roman numeral in the title. It was a sequel, but it wasn't the first. *Poltergeist* was a series, and, for a movie to get a sequel, two at that, it must be good, I imagined.

With the *Goosebumps* book under my arm, I realized just how bright the sun was, how hot the morning was getting. It was as if I had just woken up at that moment. I tugged on my Ma's shirt and described the cover.

"What's with those movies, the movies with the girl in front of stuff?"

"In front of stuff? Like a television set?"

"Yeah!"

"And she has beautiful, long, blonde hair?"

"Yeah!" I was bewildered. She seemed to catch on so quickly.

"I saw that movie when I was a bit older than you are now."

I tried to do my best impression of a puppy.

"I think you're ready for them. We'll pick up a copy from the mall later this week. You know how Papote hates the mall, especially on the weekends."

She told me the VHS might have been too old, too exposed to the sun, and battered in the travel from the vendor's large plastic tubs to the wooden tables and back into the tubs. "I'd be surprised if any of these tapes played beyond the minute mark," she said.

I had to wait.

I pestered and poked until Ma picked a date for us to visit the mall. In the meantime, I went to the internet, learning anything I could about the film, save for the plot details. The film was cursed! The skeleton used in the film was real! This movie was made by the same guy who made *E.T.*! The director of *The Texas Chainsaw Massacre*—what's that?—also directed this movie! Could I contain myself until we went to the mall?

The day came, and school felt endless. The clock's hands purposefully went as slowly as possible out of jealousy. I couldn't care less about the lessons of that day; all I wanted to do was consume *Poltergeist*. When the final bell rang, I rummaged through my locker, grabbed whatever I needed for the weekend in haste, and zoomed past the hallway monitors, the teachers, and through the double doors, frantically searching for Ma's car. She waved me down, grinning. Off to the mall we went!

On the car ride there, I pelted Ma with questions which I would quickly retract out of fear of spoiling the film mere hours before I was able to watch it. Ma just stared ahead at the road, chuckling over my eagerness.

Holding her hand, I led her to Suncoast or Sam Goody. I cannot remember which store exactly, as they sat side-by-side. Regardless, they are both relics of the past that I miss dearly.

Ma purchased the entire 3-film franchise for me. I was going to watch the first one that night!

"Are you going to watch it with me?"

"I think this is something you should experience by yourself."

With the lights dimmed, a plethora of tasty snacks in front of me, and a blanket that could serve as a shield if things became too frightening, I was ready to undertake the next part of my horror journey.

It would be an outright lie to say I wasn't scared, that I didn't peer through fingers as Marty ripped his own face from his greasy skull, as a tree came alive and snatched poor Robbie Freeling from his bed, or when Tangina screeched at the top of her lungs in an effort to guide Carol Anne and Diane through the supernatural chaos that engulfed their California home. But there was something else to the film that resonated above the chills and thrills: the bond shared between Diane and her daughter, Carol Anne. It was a ghost story, yes, but a ghost story with heart, with love, with a happy ending...until the sequel. It was a story about a mother risking it all to ensure the safety of her child.

I left the room a new person, finally having a legitimate horror film under my belt. Ma asked what I thought of the film, and I answered by hugging her with all my strength, thanking her for the gift she bestowed upon me.

*   *   *

Perhaps I was too ignorant of the outside world when I chose to be open about who I was, but Ma knew the truth that lay beyond our hedges. A mother always knows, for a mother is always right. Just because her love did not waver for me did not mean those outside of our home would have a similar outlook.

Ma's fears were not unfounded, and her worry was as valid as Gospel. I was in danger, in danger of being made the butt of a joke, of being hurt, or being a victim of a poor mindset.

Like Diane before her, Ma would do anything and everything to keep me safe, but she couldn't be everywhere with me. Diane wasn't beside Carol Anne when she was snatched by the spirits; she wasn't able to hold Carol Anne's hand while she was aimlessly walking on the Other Side. Ma couldn't sit in algebra with me or walk beside me at the mall with my friends every Saturday like an adult mallrat. I know she wished she could, but it was not logical.

What Ma was able to do was equip me with love, much like Diane did with Carol Anne. With strength, with courage, with bravery, I was able to find my way through the dark. I was as prepared to battle the Beast as I was ready to take on any smart remark made under a hot breath. I could traverse the Other Side as confidently as I could walk down a crowded hall. I could do it all, following my mother's voice back to the safety of her arms.

Author Bio

Luis Johanna Nieves was born in Moca, Puerto Rico. Currently, he teaches English language arts at the secondary level. He lives with his dog, Toby, and his partner, Anthony, in Pennsylvania.

Castrationsploitation!
Louise Weard

The first penis mutilation depicted on film was in the short animation, *Eveready Harton in Buried Treasure* (Anonymous, 1929), in which the titular character shoots off his penis, has it squeezed by a crab, and impaled by cacti. Eighty-three years later, another animated film, the anthology *Where the Dead Go To Die* (Screamerclauz, 2012), has a scene in its opening segment in which a Labrador bites off a man's penis while the dog recites a satanic prayer. In both of these examples (from animated films, no less!), the mutilation of the phallus is used as a form of exploitation with the purpose of shocking the viewers. Specifically, the act of phallic genital mutilation distresses the audience by exploiting their inherent fear of castration. The dream space of the cinema is able to amplify the symbolic power of the innate *castration anxiety*, which, although now controversial to apply in a psychoanalytic context, can be used to powerful subconscious effect when depicted on-screen.

The shocking content of *Eveready* is meant to propel the audience to laugh through their discomfort, using the genital trauma as puns that allude to male sexual anxieties. For example, the snapping crab is a metaphor for pubic lice. Although *Eveready* exists as a juvenile and transgressive joke to serve an audience mainly consisting of its animators, phallic genital mutilation has lasted as a punchline to be mocked in mainstream American comedies, including *There's Something About Mary* (Farrelly, 1998) and *21 Jump Street* (Lord & Miller,

2012).[12] In the latter example, the image of the destroyed genitalia factors into one of three overarching modes in which castration imagery is used in cinema: castration as punishment.

This first mode encompasses films in which the penis-having victim is emasculated by the Other, and several examples of self-imposed castration, for which the value of these depictions rests in communicating the symbolic fulfillment of the Freudian castration fantasy. The most common of this form is present in the rape-and-revenge exploitation subgenre, such as the bathtub castration in *I Spit On Your Grave* (Zarchi, 1978), the castration via fellatio in *The Last House on the Left* (Craven, 1972), and the surgical removal of the two rapists' testicles in Vera Chytilova's *Traps* (1998). The castration of the rapist attempts to satisfy the female victim's *penis envy*, as the ultimate revenge for the rape victim in these films is the ability to claim their assailant's phallus by translating it into their own reclaimed power as the aggressor; however, in the rape-and-revenge film the victim can never truly possess the power of the male-coded object, and it is in that lack that she can never truly find catharsis in her pursuit of revenge—at the very least if she cannot claim the power of the man than she can at least make it so that the rapist is not-all-a-man by delivering on his innate castration anxiety.

In Chytilova's film, the victim castrates her rapists to guarantee their future impotence, and although her life entropies from the fallout of her traumatic sexual assault,

---

[12] In *There's Something About Mary* Ben Stiller rips his scrotum open after catching it in his zipper and in *21 Jump Street* the heroes sever the villain's penis and he is forced to pick it up with his mouth.

she temporarily finds comfort in the idea of her eunuchs being stripped of their *jouissance* even as the judicial system fails her.[13] This posits a Lacanian view of the castration complex, which is echoed in the self-inflicted castration scenes in films like *Little Children* (Field, 2006), *American Guinea Pig: Sacrifice* (Rouge, 2017), and *The Last Woman* (Ferreri, 1976).

In these examples, the self-castrating men perform the act as an exuberant symbol of their inability to reconcile their lack of complete *jouissance*, so their innate castration becomes literal in the cinema's space of fantasy.[14] In the former, the pedophile removes his gonads because children are inaccessible as a sexual partner. In *Sacrifice,* the man removes his genitals during a transcendent pain ritual to prove himself to the goddess Ishtar, and in the Ferreri film, we witness Gerard Depardieu removing his penis with a carving knife as a response to his symbolic castration by the feminine Other, who has sought her *joiussance* outside

---

[13] *Jouissance* is a sort of extreme paradoxical pleasure, one which is of such impossible enjoyment as to be intolerable in its level of excitation. If Freud's pleasure principle provides for a limit on enjoyment to the lowest possible amount of tension, then *jouissance* is the fundamentally transgressive act of striving for and accessing forbidden pleasure—*all of the thing.* Phallic *jouissance* expresses the idea that all men are inherently castrated because they are aware of the symbol of the penis but unable to unlock its full potential because of that awareness that it could be taken away, as signified by the feminine Other.

[14] Also included in this subcategory is when the wooden block is slammed down on Willem Dafoe's cock in *Antichrist* (von Trier, 2009) as the punishment for the display of sexual ecstasy that killed their child. His penis ejaculating blood instead of seed is a transgressive symbol to highlight his distance from the unrestricted sexuality of the mythical primal horde father.

of the phallic order and is more liberated than he could ever be (and her response to seeing this pitiful man after performing the act: laughter at his expense!).

Inversely, castration is used by Oshima Nagisa in *In the Realm of the Senses* (1976) as the only suitable symbol to demonstrate Sada Abe's feminine *jouissance*, as within the inherently phallic language of cinema a male director can only show the excess of that liberated Other at the imaginary level—in this case, a penis being removed with scissors, and then carried around in Sada's pocket as Oshima has demonstrated that she is not-all subjected to the phallic order.[15]

Outside of the Freudian complex, castration as punishment is also used to symbolize the psychology of colonial violence in works such as *Dead Presidents* (Hughes & Hughes, 1995), *Candyman* (Rose, 1990), *The Serpent and the Rainbow* (Craven, 1988) and *El Topo* (Jodorowsky, 1970), as well as emphasize the cruelty and dehumanization of fascist power in *Salo, or the 120 Days of Sodom* (Pasolini, 1975), *Caligula* (Brass, 1979), *Ilsa, She Wolf of the SS* (Edmonds, 1975), and *Killer Condom* (Walz, 1996)[16].

At its most basic level, the use of castration imagery is outrageous and *sickening*, as the audience's reception to such imagery is intended to be characterized by an innate

---

[15] See also, the sexual awakening through castration using *vagina dentata* in *Lady Terminator* (Djalil, 1989) and *Teeth* (Lichtenstein, 2007), and the Other's ecstasy in performing the act shared by the leads of *Cutting Moments* (Buck, 1997) and *Cannibal* (Dora, 2006).

[16] At the end of *Killer Condom* it is revealed that the penis-eating condom creatures are the creation of a religious fundamentalist who is using them to target prostitutes, homosexuals, and transsexuals.

and sincere affective reaction of disgust. Culturally ingrained ideas of what is supposed to shock the audience encourage them to performatively share in their reaction to that which they agree should inspire disgust in them.[17] For example, in Ryan Nicholson's film *Gutterballs* (2008), scenes of bad taste, from its opening moments of transphobic harassment through to its excessively graphic gang rape sequence and elaborate murder set-pieces, all encourage the audience to collectively gag and express shock at the increasingly brutal horrors on display. While viewer reception will differ at a singular level based on individual experiences in terms of what may be considered most shocking to each audience member, a *sick film* will relish in transgressing cultural taboos in order to fulfill its maximum potential to disgust. While not all viewers will be equally disgusted at scenes of the trans woman being sexually harassed and called slurs in *Gutterballs*, the centerpiece kill in which that woman is violently castrated in extreme close-up crosses a threshold which allows for its innate *sick* qualities to be collectively reacted to at a similarly heightened level.[18]

---

[17] "Our goal is to demonstrate how these receptions [of *sick films*] are characterized equally by sincere, affective reactions of disgust and outrage as well as by self-reflexive modes of performative reception in the negotiation of the phenomenal experience of moments of abjection, impurity, and grotesquerie." *Cult Cinema* (Ernest Mathijs & Jamie Sexton, 2011), page 106.

[18] Jorg Buttgereit's *Schramm* (1993) is an another example of castration used in the *sick film*; the main character hammers three nails into his penis in close-up—a pure and purposefully transgressive image, the uncompromising focus on the destruction being intercut with his sexually violent fantasies.

In castrationsploitation films, the abjection of the sight of the malformed or destroyed penis, as well as the act of its destruction, must be reacted to, and the degree of rejection or catharsis in that reaction varies based on the audience's perception of perpetrator and victim. Thus, castration can be found being executed as the ultimate punishment granted towards or by the repressed Other in all manner and subgenre of exploitation films, the earliest example of which is in the lost ending of *Freaks* (Browning, 1930) in which Hercules is castrated by the titular performers and is then witnessed singing as a tenor on-stage. From martial arts films[19] to blaxploitation,[20] cannibals[21] to mondo,[22] since Jodorowsky introduced it in the first true Midnight Movie of the 1970s, castration has become the defining symbol of exploitation cinema.

This leads us to our second application of castration imagery: meta-castrationsploitation. An exploitation throwback film such as *Grindhouse* (Tarantino, Rodriguez, et al., 2006) defines its *cult film* status using self-conscious intertextual references, with castration imagery being an obvious use of empty citation to place it within this space. The opening scene of Rodriguez's installment features a military guard having his testicles removed as the consequence for failing his employer, which recalls the mob boss violently castrating an underling who wronged

---

[19] *The Street Fighter* (Ozawa, 1974), *Bruce Lee Against Superman* (Chun, 1975)

[20] *Foxy Brown* (Hill, 1974), *Welcome Home Brother Charles* (Fanaka, 1975)

[21] *Emanuelle and the Last Cannibals* (D'Amato, 1977), *Cannibal Ferox* (Lenzi, 1981), *Cannibal Holocaust* (Deodato, 1980)

[22] *Goodbye Uncle Tom* (Jacopetti & Prosperi, 1971)

him in the opening scene of *Ricco the Mean Machine* (Demicheli, 1973). Films such as *Father's Day* (Astron-6. 2011), *Hobo With A Shotgun* (Eisener, 2011), and *Death Drop Gorgeous* (Ahern, Dalpe, & Perras, 2021), amongst a swath of other films in the Neo-exploitation movement, use castration self-reflexively in order to canonize themselves through their awareness of on-screen castration as a defining marker of exploitation cinema. Even if one of these films is classifiable within other subgenres of exploitation, it is through the intertextual conversation of penis mutilation that a glossy Millennial horror film like *Hostel: Part II* (Roth, 2007) encourages the audience to recall the earlier torture-film *Bloodsucking Freaks* (Reed, 1976), satisfying Roth's attempt to place his wide-release film within the context of exploitation film history.

In these works, on-screen castration often becomes an easily definable shorthand that post-modern filmmakers use as empty citation, one-degree separated from the symbolic significance of *castration as punishment* imagery and diluted into a slurry of meta-textual self-servicing in which the director provides the viewer with satisfaction for recognizing their reference—a mutual catharsis among fans and fans-turned-filmmakers.[23] *Female Prisoner Scorpion: Jailhouse 41* (Ito, 1972) features an extremely graphic scene in which a prison guard's genitalia is impaled by a large mast of wood, then Meiko Kaji's iconic outfit is prominently featured in Sion Sono's *Love Exposure* (2008) which features a graphic castration scene of its own. However, with its rampant cross-dressing and

---

[23] For example, Tarantino's *Pulp Fiction* (1994) defines its rape-revenge scene by its intertextual awareness of the gory shotgun blast to the testicles in *House on the Edge of the Park* (Deodato, 1980).

gender confusion, Sono's film transcends the *meta*-category and places itself within the third context of castration imagery: transgender readings of castration imagery.

A transgender reading of on-screen castration imagery begins with the silver screen's fascination with the surgical castration, introduced in Ed Wood's *Glen or Glenda* (1953), which exploited the media's fascination with trans woman Christine Jorgensen and opened the door for the transploitation mini-movement of the 1960s.[24] Although the surgery is recreated offscreen in Wood's film, the film relishes in its allusive descriptions ("Then comes the removal of the man!"). This subversive crossing of the gender binary provides the exploitation angle to these early transploitation films, with the primary mode of spectatorship relegated to a primitive *cinema of attractions* or mondo style. Viewers are invited to behold the spectacle of the transgender body (oftentimes portrayed by cis actors)—the poster of Andy Milligan's *Fleshpot on 42nd Street* even challenges its audience as to whether they can identify a trans woman: "Both are hustlers...but one is a male. Guess which?" Regarding the surgical castration films of this period, to a cisgender viewer the shock of watching Doris Wishman's *Let Me Die A Woman!* is in its medical context since the familiarity of surgical *healing* is transgressed by the unfamiliar reassignment and the foreignness of the transgender body. However, a

---

[24] *She-Man: A Story of Fixation* (Clark, 1967), *I Was A Man* (Mahon, 1967), *The Christine Jorgensen Story* (Rapper, 1970), *I Want What I Want* (Dexter, 1972), *Let Me Die A Woman!* (Wishman, 1978), *Fleshpot on 42nd Street* (Milligan, 1973), *Sex and Violence* (aka *Ensalada Baudelaire*, Pomés, 1977)

transgender viewer may find catharsis in some of the better examples that capture the experience of dysphoria and can understand (if not empathize with) the symbolic healing inherent to the act of self-castration at the conclusion of *I Want What I Want* (as opposed to the mondo approach of Wishman's dysphoria-induced self-castration segment).

In the climax of *I Want What I Want*, a potential suitor of lead character Wendy[25] is overcome by *trans panic* after discovering her penis during their unexpected tryst and violently throws her into a mirror. Taking a shard of the broken mirror in her hand, she castrates herself before the film cuts to a year later as she wakes up from her confirmation surgery. The film uses castration as a liberating device for its trans character, cutting from the bloody scene of dysphoria to that of Wendy experiencing gender *euphoria*, proudly whispering her name after hearing it said by the surgeon and declaring, "I must remember how lucky I am to be a girl" as the camera zooms out from her apartment window to reveal a sunny day.

A far more exploitative example of gender dysphoria alongside a symbolic castration is depicted in Bob Clark's schlocky *She-Man: A Story of Fixation*. Albert is the cis American everyman who is blackmailed into being forcibly feminized by drag queen Dominita via means of hormone therapy and cross-dressing. The horror of the film is in how Albert must now experience dysphoria as his body changes, and he is socially misgendered as "Rose" in Dominita's *gender-freak* estate; when told to wear a maid

---

[25] Portrayed empathetically by cis actress, Anne Heywood, which is notable for a transploitation film considering that trans women have been predominantly played by cis men throughout the history of their "representation" on-screen.

uniform, he protests, "I won't let her turn me into any drag queen!" and the film emphasizes the horror of having his eyebrows plucked with a shocking stinger piercing the score. Upon seeing himself in the mirror, he exclaims, "Why God?" and expresses horror at how the estrogen has changed his body, yet by the end of the film, the narrator says that Albert has found that he enjoys cross-dressing with his bisexual partner in the bedroom.[26]

Albert reconciles his brush with gender experimentation within the confines of a binary cissexual hegemony, a sexual fetish that can be performed in private. Dominita does not receive the same gender-experimentation approval, as after being outed by Albert, her *gender-freaks* turn on her in an homage to Tod Browning's film, stripping her naked and taking away her signature whip (which the narrator carefully explains was the symbol of her domineering power).[27]

Nearly a century after the first (lost) castration scene in Tod Browning's *Freaks*, Lloyd Kaufman's *#Shakespeare'sShitstorm* (2020) features an on-screen castration of a man pulling off his own dick during an orgy of transformation, culminating in Kaufman's Prospero presenting the audience with his own *freakish* transformation (including multiple sets of genitalia, a

---

[26] This idea of forced-feminization is used as the ironic, horrifying punchline to *Frankenhooker* (Henenlotter, 1990), as the murderous mad scientist Jeffrey is placed in a female body and screams from his experiencing of gender dysphoria, imitating Frankenstein as he touches where his penis used to be.

[27] Castrating a person in drag as revenge also occurs in John Waters' *Pink Flamingos* (1972), in which the captive pregnant women emasculate Channing after being freed by Divine.

surgically attached and *appropriated* new penis and vagina). The reaction by the guests of the orgy is a celebration of the character's body horror transformation as *transition*, complete with assertions of "You're so brave!" The explicit horror and irony of the reaction is a complete reversal of the reaction in Browning's film; in the omitted scene in *Freaks*, Venus's reaction to the fate of Cleo and Hercules is one of shock and pity, while in Kaufman's film the transformation is celebrated in an ironic commentary on cultural *wokeness* and the commodified infantilization of transgender bodies. While Cleo is shot from a pitifying high angle, trapped in the sideshow pit to be observed by the voyeuristic crowd and viewer, Prospero goes on the talk-show circuit, his transformed body becoming a different kind of commodity for a modern-day, culturally accepted freakshow.

In nearly a century of horror films, the mix of transformation, castration, and the transgender body's depiction on-screen hasn't changed beyond the ability to show increasingly explicit gore, but the mode of the *freakshow* certainly has. The difference between the agony of the sideshow pit in *Freaks* and the talk-show dressing room in which Prospero puts on make-up is little more than an air of respectability in the latter; however, both institutions seek to profit from the spectacle of the transgender body perceived by a privileged cisgender audience—*Freaks'* carnival barker finds its Troma equivalent in Oprah.[28]

---

[28] Look no further than Sam Feder's documentary *Disclosure* (2020) to find a catalogue of uncomfortable-looking trans women being asked whether they got "the surgery" on national television as examples of this castration fascination as populist spectacle.

In direct opposition to these examples of castration as gender-affirmation is Doris Wishman's *The Amazing Transplant* (1970). In the film, shy and involuntarily celibate Arthur has a back-alley abortionist surgically replace his penis with that of his recently deceased friend Felix; the reason for this penile re-assignment, Arthur is jealous of Felix's liberated sexual appetites—unlike Arthur, he is not even afraid to get girls pregnant. The story plays out as an exploitation version of *Orlac's Hands* (Weine, 1924) as Arthur discovers that the previous owner of his penis was a serial rapist triggered by a fetish for gold earrings, turning the once shy character into a violent rapist and murderer. Similarly to the following penis transplant film, *Percy* (Thomas, 1971), the symbolic power of transplanting a better penis over the previously non-functioning (or, in *Percy*'s case, mutilated by a chandelier) member is in its ability to bring the male subject closer to the complete *jouissance* of Freud's primal horde father. This figure is the exception to the innate castration complex, which has limited sexual access to all women, and it is in the penis transplant that these men are able to *un-castrate* themselves and pursue complete sexual satisfaction (within the framework of the film's narrative universes).[29]

The equation of the penile reassignment leading to the previously *normal* character becoming violent echoes outwards to the depiction of trans masculine character Max Sweeney on *The L Word* (Chaiken, Abbott, & Greenberg, 2004-2009), who becomes increasingly violent after beginning testosterone therapy. The depiction of masculine

[29] *Sex and Zen* (Mak, 1991) pushes this concept to its extreme, featuring a transplant of a 20-inch horse cock which allows its bearer to sexually access any partner he wishes.

transition on-screen is so rooted in this transphobic concept that to become *un-castrated* is to become a danger towards all women.[30] At the end of Wishman's film, Arthur expresses regret for ever having the idea of getting the surgery and begs for a way to *de-transition*, and after turning himself in, is found Not Guilty for his crimes while under the control of the phallus. Conversely, in John Waters' *Desperate Living* (1977), the penis transplant sought out by Mole to please their girlfriend is met with abject horror as they discover how far the transplant is from the *real thing* and reject the facsimile by cutting it off in a painful over-the-top display of dysphoria.[31]

The *Orlac's Hands* narrative also inspires Alejandro Jodorowsky's *Santa Sangre* (1989), in which, after witnessing the castration of his father at the hands of his mother, Fenix becomes the arms of his amputated mother and carries out her revenge. At the end, it is revealed that Fenix's mother has only existed in his trauma-induced delusions, and he himself has been playing the role of his mother, reminiscent of *Psycho* (Hitchcock, 1960). After rejecting the control which his mother possessed over his body, Fenix emerges from the ruins of his mother's temple to discover that he now has agency over his body, expressing euphoria at the prospect of raising his hands

---

[30] In some cases the on-screen castration cannot even prevent rape or violence towards women, such as in *Grindhouse* when Tarantino's soldier is unhindered even as his testicles and penis begin to melt off.

[31] Another rejection of the phallus occurs in Frank Henenlotter's *Bad Biology* (2008), as Batz wishes his once surgically re-attached penis would stay off of his body for good so that he can continue to live (his penis is literally killing him), but instead it kills him when Jennifer uses it to reach an orgasm akin to being "fucked by God," feminine *jouissance*.

while declaring, "*My* hands." The young boy witnessing his father's castration and then becoming subjected to the control of the *not-all-castrated* feminine body as he matures into an adult before taking steps to self-actualize by affirming his gender at the end of the film provides for a beautiful closing image of trans masculine euphoria as the camera rises up with Fenix's nail-polish-free hands.

Love Exposure also ends with the expression of gender euphoria, as Yû accidentally sees her panty-bulge for the first time and snaps out of her trauma-induced psychosis. Her condition prior to her self-actualization is the result of the story's villain, Aya, who is shown castrating her abusive father's erect penis in graphic close-up with a pair of scissors followed by a geyser of blood. Aya becomes obsessed with Yû after witnessing her status as a contradictory gender-confused mess and proceeds to torture Yû using her knowledge of Yû's alter-ego Miss Scorpion, threatening to out her to Yû's romantic interest Yoko.[32] Yû's psychosis is induced when she is outed as Miss Scorpion in front of Yoko, and Aya commits suicide, having realized how far Yû is from some idealized version of a castrated man which she has imagined since she castrated her father—not a trans woman, but a perfectly repressed *safe* man, who has accepted his innate castration without neurosis. At the conclusion of the film, Yû internalizes the alter-ego of Miss Scorpion through the

---

[32] In Yoko's introduction an emphasis is placed on her worship of Kurt Cobain, a notable cross-dresser.

recognition of her feminine penis,[33] reconciling it with her own agency, and is finally able to embrace Yoko as a fully realized person, with hands once again being used as *Love Exposure*'s closing image of gender euphoria.

The castration complex is set against a backdrop of religious excess and repression in Sono's film, and castration becomes ritual itself in *Where the Dead Go To Die, Der Todesking* (Buttgereit, 1990),[34] and *The Holy Mountain* (Jodorowsky, 1973). Jodorowsky's ritual castration scene is lavishly executed with vibrant colours and ornate production design, which is in stark opposition to the production values of "The Ritual ov Psychick Youth" found in Genesis P-Orridge's *First Transmission* (1982). The semi-real castration initiation ritual on the first (of four) *First Transmission* videotape is the inaugural example of on-screen castration directed by a self-identifying non-binary or transgender filmmaker.[35] In the ritual segment, a person with a penis is subjected to all sorts of abuse, culminating in a blood enema followed by their

---

[33] Sono uses the Lacanian mirror as the catalyst for Yû's self-actualization, the trans woman's recognition emerging from the coexistence of panties and untucked bulge.

[34] The Nazi-inflicted castration by shears in *Der Todesking* is paid homage to in Greg Araki's *The Doom Generation* (1995), and the blending of religious imagery (in this case, crucifixion) and castration also appears in *I Will Walk Like A Crazy Horse* (Arrabal, 1973) and *The Fourth Man* (Verhoeven, 1983).

[35] The term "first" is problematic in any transgender historical context, but in this case it is notable to share that Genesis P-Orridge and h/er partner, Lady Jaye Breyer, were *pandrogyne*, and sought to end binary interpretation of gender.

castration.[36] The nearly structuralist editing pattern cuts in flashes of frames that draw a comparison between knife-on-penis, to a woman's vagina, and back again. At the end of the segment, a partially obscured castration occurs, and after a short intermission, a hairless, genderless body appears on-screen. The figure touches a piece of fabric concealing their genitals, soundtracked to the haunting post-suicide portion of the *Jonestown Death Tape*.[37] Finally, the shroud is removed to reveal the castrated genitalia, shown in a celebratory fashion which presents their glorious transformation to the audience with a nearly transcendent poeticism; the figure seductively touches themself, Other *jouissance* achieved by castration.[38]

As a transfemme writer and director, I use the imagery of on-screen castration in my films *Computer Hearts* (2014)[39] and *S.I.D.S.* (2015) to similarly explore gender transformation through castration. In my adolescence, I was drawn to films featuring extreme body

---

[36] The cinematographer of *First Transmission*, Peter Christopherson, also directed *Nine Inch Nails: Broken* (1993), which ends with a violent on-screen castration and features a performance by Bob Flanagan, who hammered a nail into his penis in *SICK: The Life and Death of Bob Flanagan, Supermasochist* (Dick, 1997).

[37] The soundtrack adds to the cult imagery, alongside imagined "Satanic" alters and pentagrams.

[38] In the second segment, "Castration Movie," a most-likely un-simulated surgical castration is performed on a participant in which the penis is removed and then replaced with an electronic pleasure device, making it symbolically clear what Genesis P-Orridge hopes to communicate in h/er castration philosophy: castration leads to the experience of *jouissance*, and is, perhaps, *jouissance* itself.

[39] Co-directed by Dionne Copland and co-starring trans masculine actor Romijn Miller as Albert's fiancé.

horror because I increasingly felt a sense of depersonalization from my own body as it moved further away from my own perception of self. To secretly watch a pirated copy of a film such as *Guinea Pig: Flower of Flesh and Blood* (Hino, 1985) at a young age was essential to grappling with those feelings and not feeling isolated in them, as the transcendent and pleasurable bodily deconstruction experienced by the film's victim expressed a form of *jouissance* which spoke to my relationship to my transforming body to which the impossible pleasure was to take it back under my own control. I became enamoured with gory horror films and underground cinema as a means of exorcising my own internal sensation of body horror, drawn especially towards their transgressive propensity to show what was to me the ultimate taboo: castration.

For my debut film, I hired the make-up effects artist behind the notoriously transphobic castration gag in *Gutterballs*, Michelle Grady, who could not have been a more appropriate choice to bring my body horror odyssey to life. I came to know Grady after *Gutterballs* director Ryan Nicholson offered me my first job in the film industry.

I met Nicholson at a one-time horror film festival in Calgary, Alberta at the premiere of his film *Star Vehicle* (2010) when I was sixteen years old. He recognized my passion for horror cinema, and he told me that if I found my way out to Vancouver, British Columbia he would make sure I found a place on one of his movies. Years later he stayed true to his word, and I ended up having my introduction to the film industry as his assistant on *Collar* (2014). That moment was an important part of my life, being this nineteen-year-old kid getting the chance to be involved with that underground artistic community. It was the first time I got to be around other weirdos like me. I had always felt like I was such an outcast, and I really did not know what was wrong with me. Being this transgressive edgy strange person who liked all these things, it was a pretty real fear of mine that I might be institutionalized growing up. Even though at that time I still could not communicate what was wrong with me or at least unable to take the steps to deal with it, I still found catharsis in extreme and transgressive art and was now working with people who made these kinds of films. For the first time, I felt accepted in a community of artists that were just as weird as me, all in their own ways. It was a very big turning point in my life. How humorous is it that the first time I was ever perceived as a transgender woman was when Ryan Nicholson asked if I would play one as a victim in one of his films? I was far too closeted to actually go through with it. My shield of performative masculinity was so fragile as to even make the suggestion too much, but in the unreleased footage I shot as the cinematographer for the unfinished *Gutterballs 3,* you would find me in the most feminine presentation I had ever felt comfortable with before transitioning. In hindsight, that seems to be the case with many who find themselves in this work. Whatever trauma gets you there, the art is how you find catharsis and community.

So, I had Michelle Grady on board to help me with my debut film. The film combined many elements of my closeted and repressed transgender identity: an exploration of performative masculinity, depersonalization, Internet identity, and a myriad of other gender anxieties all culminating in a scene of castration. In *Computer Hearts*, Albert (played by me) creates an online avatar of his ideal woman who he becomes mutually obsessed with to the point of physical transformation. The film culminates in Albert's body being taken over by the female avatar and transformed into a half-man, half-computer, before finally assimilating him by having his penis ripped off and absorbed by the computer's vaginal disk-drive. Albert can only break free from the body-control by killing himself, and in the final shot of the film, a female hand bursts out of the disk-drive vagina, revealing that Albert's female avatar has become flesh. Although designed as a shocking jump-scare, it is another example of using hands as a film's closing image to showcase gendered self-actualization on-screen.

In my following film *S.I.D.S.*, my lead character seeks out an orchiectomy from a back-alley surgeon as an extreme reaction to paternal anxiety.[40] Once again playing the film's lead character, I brought my nightmares of fatherhood and of navigating the medical system as a transgender woman to the screen. In an intertextual twist, I cast Ryan Nicholson as the doctor who, in voice-over, denies my character gender-affirming surgery due to their uncertainty towards wanting children. When my character awakes after the back-alley surgery, their testicles are thankfully missing, but they are horrified to discover that the removed testicles have become sentient and impregnated the surgeon, who immediately explodes with an unwanted fetus. The final image of the film features the

---

[40] Similarly, the neo-exploitation film *Trannysnatchers!* (Caedmonster, Boxwell & Jamonsta, 2012) includes a scene of a back-alley vaginoplasty, albeit played in comedic fashion. The surgeon haphazardly stabs at the woman's penis before the film cuts to reveal her perfect new vagina. Her friend then pleasures her with a vibrator as she exclaims "I'm a lady!" in euphoric ecstasy.

lead character laughing at the absurd irony of their predicament, having been thwarted in their attempt to escape an expected masculine, paternal role. There is no Other *jouissance* or euphoria for the trans bodies in these films, and in the latter, it is the inability to become fully castrated from the male-assigned body which causes distress. What I instead express in these films is the pining for that feeling of *jouissance* and having it denied by a cosmically unjust world of biological gendered body fatalism. *I am a transsexual, and therefore I am a monster.*[41] The final line of *Computer Hearts* finds my character facing the blackened computer screen-as-mirror and saying, "I'm sorry." *Castration is not enough.* It is perhaps telling that I made both of these films before I transitioned.

The three modes of applying on-screen castration imagery within the framework of exploitation cinema reveal it to be a significant symbol for this mode of filmmaking, versatile in its thematic and narrative application. From the use of castration as punishment to the categorization of sick films and Neo-exploitation films which use castration as a shorthand to canonize themselves using an inherently transgressive reference source, castrationsploitation has been key to the language of exploitation cinema throughout its history—as well as appearing alongside the representation of transgender characters, stories, and themes used in a variety of contexts on-screen. Inherently, the canon of exploitation cinema is inseparable from its fixation on castration, and, thus, a transgender film analysis.

---

[41] *My Words to Victor Frankenstein Above the Village of Chamounix: Performing Transgender Rage* (Susan Stryker, 1994)

Author Bio

Louise Weard is a filmmaker with a degree in Film Semiotics. Hailing from Western Canada, she cut her teeth working as the cinematographer for FX legend Ryan Nicholson and emerged as an exciting new voice in underground horror with her breakout body-horror featurette Computer Hearts. Along with her filmmaking partner Dionne Copland, Louise established CyberCraft Video in 2016 and produced the short films *Inferno* and *Haxx Deadroom*, as well as the micro-budget queer slasher film Cuties. After film school she produced Dionne Copland's feature-length debut, the cabin-in-the-woods creature-feature Cold Wind Blowing, which was released in 2022.

She has been obsessed with deeply personal (and perverse) movies that push the envelope for as long as she can remember, which culminated in her winning a Most Fearless Performance Award in 2015 for her short film S.I.D.S. in which she played herself as a transsexual woman seeking a back-alley surgery. Nearly a decade after completing her debut film, Computer Hearts, it was rediscovered as a significant work of transgender horror cinema and screened at The Music Box in Chicago, IL during their Music Box of Horrors event with Shudder in October 2022.

Her film theory writing encompasses work on the on-screen semiotics of the Marquis de Sade and a comprehensive history of films featuring phallic genital trauma, the latter of which can be found in the book Divergent Terror: The Crossroads of Queerness and Horror. In September 2022, she co-hosted the 100 Best

Kills event at Fantastic Fest in a night dedicated to castration scenes in film.

For Louise, cinema is about illuminating the most secretive and problematic parts of the self and using storytelling to connect with other freaks and outcasts so that nobody has to feel alone. Her obsessions include ritual Magick, Gnosticism, and UFOs, and when she's not making movies you'll find her championing unsung visionary filmmakers through her film writing or her role at Fantastic Fest. She has also directed some extremely transgender-coded music videos for musical artists Ravine Angel and Magda Baker, and while filming one she may have "accidentally" performed a ritual that made her trans.

Acknowledgements

W. Dale Jordan and Off Limits Press LLC wish to thank the numerous supporters who came together to make this project a reality. From the authors to those who gave of their time helping promote the Kickstarter and all points in between, we salute you.

We would like, in particular, to give a shout-out to Samantha Kolesnik, Adam Robitel, Scary Stuff Podcast, Hope Madden, Meghan, Laura E., Eli Whisnant, and Elizabeth and Martin Nicchetta.

This book and these personal stories would not exist without your support!

CPSIA information can be obtained
at www.ICGtesting.com
Printed in the USA
BVHW072113151222
654331BV00023B/1630